innovative
houses

Author: Arian Mostaedi
Publishers: Carles Broto & Josep Mª Minguet
Editorial Coordination: Jacobo Krauel
Architecture Adviser: Pilar Chueca
Graphic Design & Production: Héctor Navarro
Layout: Daniel Álvarez
Text: Contributed by the architects, edited by
Jacobo Krauel and Amber Ockrassa

© Cover photograph: Kim Zwarts
ISBN: 84-89861-35-8
D.L.: 41477-2003

Printed in Barcelona, Spain

© Links International
Jonqueres, 10. 1-5
08003 Barcelona, Spain
Tel.: +34 93 301 21 99
Fax: +34 93 301 00 21

innovative
houses

index

introduction

To innovate means introducing the unprecedented; it means throwing out the rule book, ignoring what you have always understood to be the "right" or "wrong" way to do things. Innovation means always striving for something new.

On the following pages, you'll find that this restless will to innovate may appear in any number of forms. Some architects experiment with a reworking of shape, materials or context. See, for example, the enclosed, pod-like studio sitting in the middle of a spacious London loft, or the spectacular home set between sheer concrete walls surrounded by ranch-homes in Arizona. Elsewhere, a trapezoid sits where the eye expects a square; or the modernity of a loft is unexpectedly integrated into a cozy cottage-like home; or a massive glass-house comprises an entire façade.

We also find ingenuity put to use in coming up with ecologically sound solutions. One studio decided to leave the site's original pine trees in place, opting instead to include them as an integral part of the layout of a light-filled, bay-side home in France. And, as an example of one of the more spectacular, earth-friendly solutions is the colorful "Ecological House of the Future", with its energy-generating windmills and water purification systems gracefully integrated into a home filled with plants, ponds and waterfalls. Other architects find their voices in the face of adversity, coming up with new solutions to especially difficult sites (one studio closed off views toward the dull surroundings, opening the house up to skyward panoramas instead) or overcoming zoning restrictions in creative ways.

Whatever the case may be, we trust that this selection of some of the finest, most innovative architectural solutions in the world will serve as an endless source of inspiration. Enjoy!

PAUHOF Architekten
House P
Gramastetten, Austria

Though opposed and repeatedly denied building permit by the local environment protection agency, both the architects and the clients stuck tenaciously to their guns and finally succeeded in building this house (which went on to win the "OÖ Landeskulturpreis" cultural award) to its original specification. Neither the problems encountered during building (which took more than three years) nor the need to find ad hoc solutions enabling the owner and families to build the house in their spare time using their own resources, compromised the team´s commitment to the original design or the technical standard of construction. The building, which makes no typological or linguistic concessions to traditional Austrian rural architecture, is profoundly linked to the typology of its site by sensitive down-slope configuration, skilfully contrived views from the interior and manipulation of natural light. The subtly controlled contrasts and interpretations of inside and outside, evident at once from a tour of the interior and exterior spaces, are the result of uncompromising theoretical precision distilled over the years from unrealized large-scale projects, architectural installations and temporary exhibition designs. The big horizontal window to one side of the main entrance immediately reveals the ambiguous nature of the concrete wall which encloses the garden and the pergola delimiting the open-air "room", the only designed exterior space, levelled and visually integrated with the house to form a spatial continuum. It unfurls to contain the entire ground floor volume, before extending conceptually and physically into space as a glass strip, the source of natural light for the basement level. The ground floor´s tendency toward static abstraction is explicity confirmed by the suspended prism of the upper floor and the choice of materials: bare, porous concrete to anchor the building to the ground, and clinical-looking, polished aluminum cladding to emphasize the abstract isolation of the suspended upper volume. The construction concept systematically developed in previous PAUHOF projects is evident only inside the building in the daring static design of the suspended volume containing the sleeping quarters: a pillar and a wall which rises through all three levels, stabilizing the entire building. The abstractness of the external volumes is ameliorated inside by warm colors and a new set of textures. Inside the house, other containers are superimposed on the basic concrete structural container. They include the oak lobby-box of the main entrance, the furniture-box separating the kitchen and the dining area, the kitchen-box extending outwards to the garden and, on the basement level, the fragmented box formed by the waxed oak floor, wall cladding and bookshelves.

Photographs: Matteo Piazza

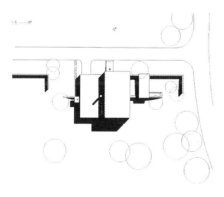

Site plan

The abstraction of the external volumes, emphasized by monochrome colors that eliminate the contrast between the textures of the aluminum and concrete, is replaced in the interior by warm colors and new textures.

Axonometric view

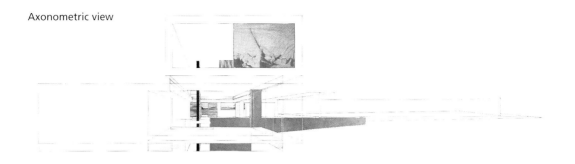

Section

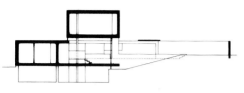

Elevation

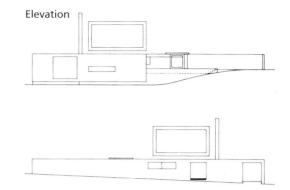

Ground floor plan

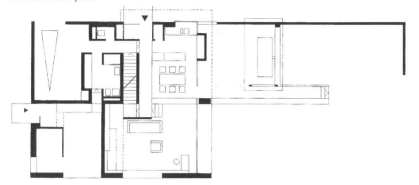

First floor plan

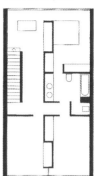

Construction details

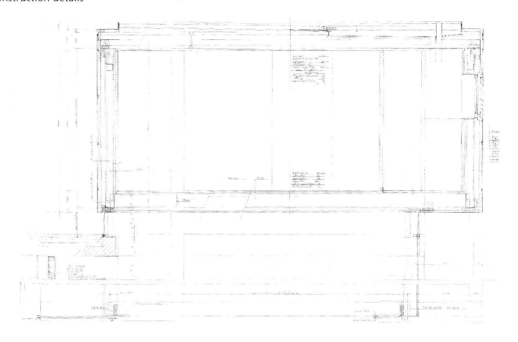

Inside the dwelling, other volumes are superimposed on the concrete structural container. These include the oak-clad hall of the main entrance, the element that separates the kitchen from the dining room, the extension of the box of the kitchen toward the garden and, in the basement, the fragmented box formed by the waxed oak floor, metal-clad walls and shelves.

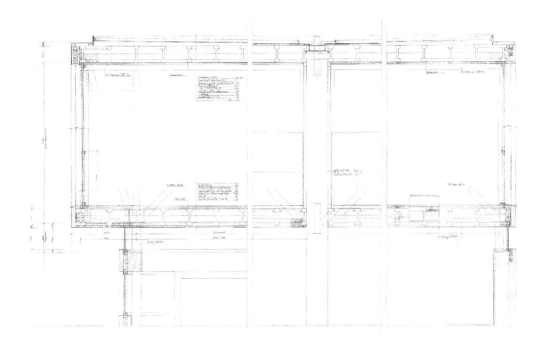

Eugeen Liebaut
Verhaeghe House
Sint Pieters Leeuw, Belgium

The program for this house near Brussels was chosen from among ten competing architectural studios. The Verhaeghe house is a simple two-story structure with a flat roof, hemmed in on both sides by neighboring buildings. Since the site itself was seven meters wide and zoning restrictions would only allow a height of six meters, a modest volume had to be designed.

With such spatial restrictions, the architects decided to make room by sinking the ground floor 80cm to the level of the foundation masonry. Financially, this is a simple enough operation; while the advantages gained in spatial configuration are highly attractive. The living room is a high-ceilinged, transparent space. Here, the inhabitants move freely about between two strategically-placed volumes –the kitchen and the toilet– which do not reach the full height of the ceiling. Together, these volumes form a screen of sorts within the transparent volume which provides the necessary privacy from the public street. The high and wide glass facade rises from an incision between the volume and the socle like a rare and floating object.

The rear facade is also entirely glazed, making the steel-grated terrace outside seem like a continuation of the dwelling. By working with grates, the bedrooms on the ground floor are ensured sufficient light. This relatively small house enjoys a spatiality of which many a majestic villa can only dream.

Photographs: Saskia Vanderstichele

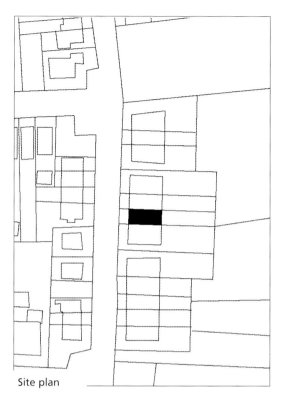

Site plan

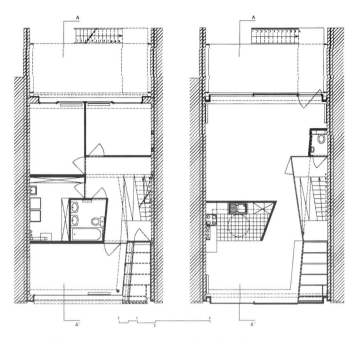

Ground floor plan   First floor plan

Since zoning restrictions required a height of no more than 6 meters, interior space was gained by sinking the house by nearly one meter.

The block containing the kitchen is positioned to shield the interior from views from the street.

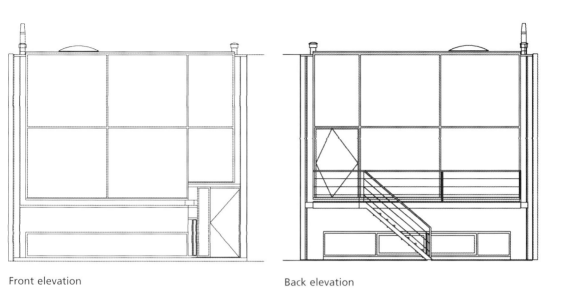

Front elevation

Back elevation

Shin Takamatsu & Associates
Iwai House
Minami-ku, Kyoto. Japan

Alone in open fields on the edge of town, in an almost defenseless site beyond an industrial belt, stands this two-story house, built in reinforced concrete with a steel frame. On both interior and exterior, the architects have brought to bear all the expressive potential of concrete.

The most eye-catching feature of the exterior is the curved wall alongside the entrance on the main facade. At first glance this convex wall seems rather aggressive, but within the residence its concavity becomes intimate.

The curved wall also forms the outer edge of a secluded courtyard, and incorporates a raised walkway and a terrace form which one can contemplate the scenery. The courtyard and the large windows overlooking it are protected by a brise-soleil.

The glazed entrance hall leads into a curving corridor in which the untreated structural concrete creates a fine visual balance with the wooden flooring. Concrete is left unadorned throughout much of the house, for example in the columns, and complements the plastered surfaces, largely in white with patches of primary colors.

The home's interior is completely modern, although it owes a great deal of its delicacy to traditional Japanese aesthetics. The atrium leading to the terrace is a good example of the common ground that exists between the two approaches.

Photographs: Nacása & Partners

Site plan

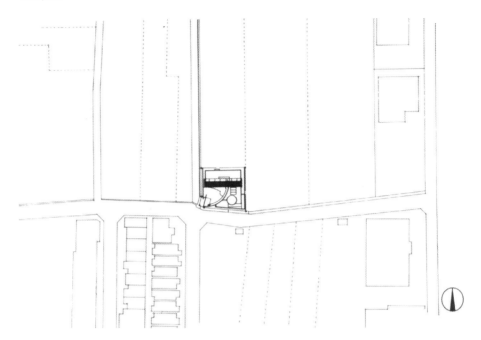

Main facade drawing

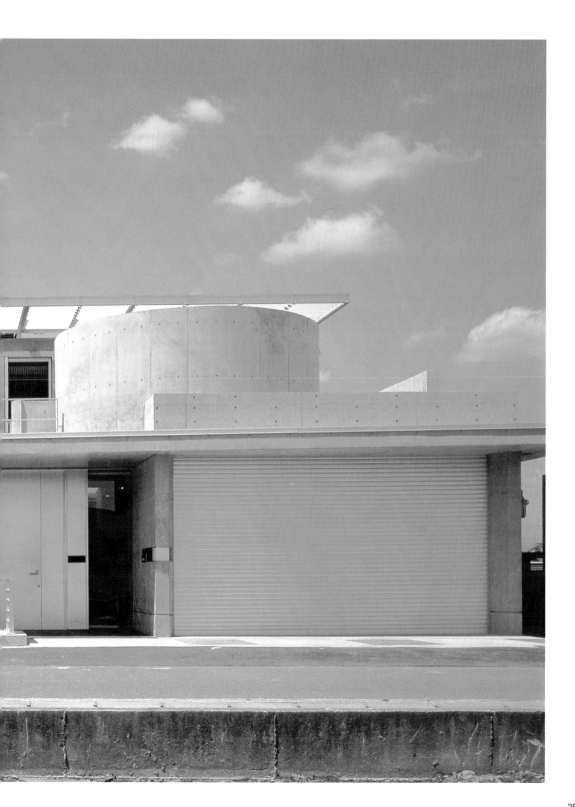

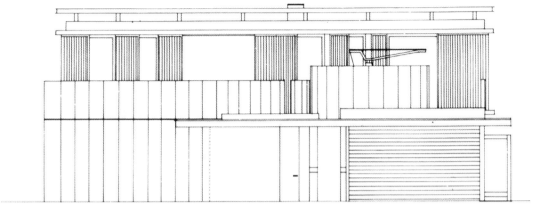

South elevation

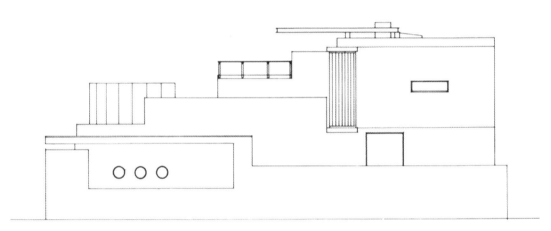

East elevation

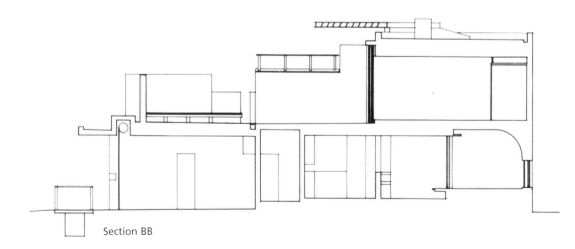

Section BB

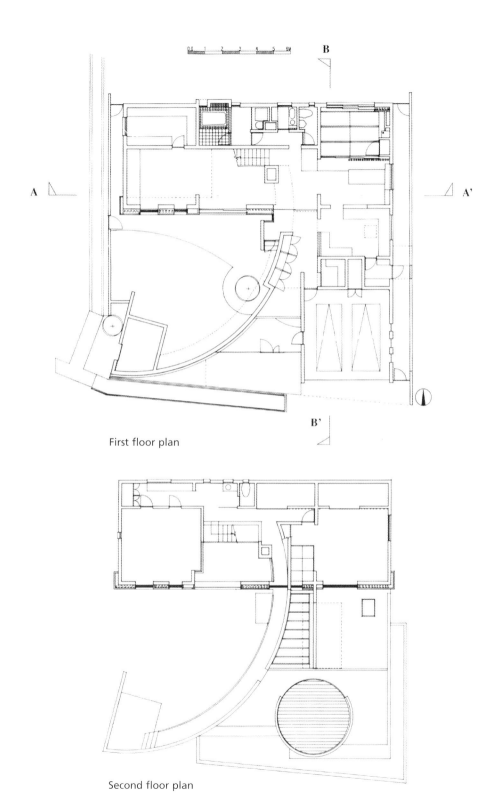

First floor plan

Second floor plan

The interior design combines industrial production and traditional detail, rough material and finishes in primary colors.
The architect recreated a typically Oriental atmosphere of serenity in some of the rooms to take refuge from the chaos of Kyoto's outskirts.

Hermann & Valentiny et Associès
Haus am seitweg
Klosterneuburg, Austria

This house sits on a relatively steep incline in the midst of several other standard single family houses and provides a significant alternative to the ever popular gable roof seen in the surrounding area. The sixty degree slope of the roof's concrete slab stands as a visual metaphor, albeit a contemporary one. The lamella skin on the west facade, which casts a comforting shadow onto a deck-like terrace in the afternoon, also contributes to setting the building's exterior appearance apart from the rest.

By contrast, the interior concept is very simple. From the street, one enters the dwelling on the floor where a very open living room and kitchen are located. A steep staircase leads from here to the client's workspace and to a spare bedroom. The master and children's bedrooms, each of which enjoys direct access to the garden, are located below.

The home's rigorous limitation of materials (naked concrete with inherent "painterly" flaws, wood, glass, and, in the bathroom, Eternit) makes a pleasant impression.

The views within the house are also soothing, from the entrance to the children's rooms. The outward-facing orientation, with a wide panoramic view offered to the occupants, is particularly spectacular.

Photographs: G.G. Kirchner

Site plan

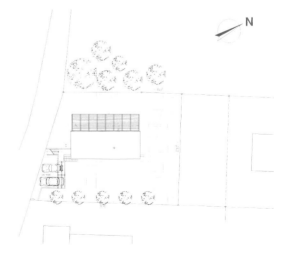

Limestone was used for the exterior cladding. The contrast between this and the white of the roof endows this structure with a dynamic, innovative character.

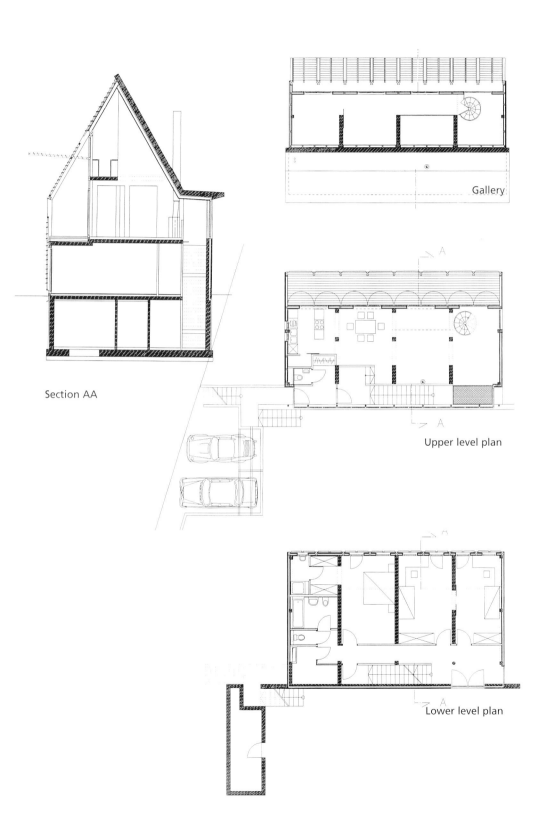

Section AA

Gallery

Upper level plan

Lower level plan

The glazing of one of the slopes of the gable roof has allowed the architects to infuse the home's interior with natural light and views.

Section details

Holzrahmen 8x8 mit Holzlamellen-Lärchenholz
Leimbinder-Lärchenholz 15x25

TERRASSE

Holzriegelwand-hinterlüftete Fassade

WOHNEN

HORIZONTALSCHNITT-ANSCHLUSS HOLZRIEGELWAND/LEIMBINDER

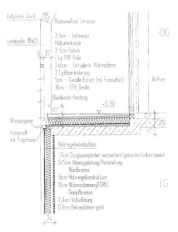

Fußpfette 12x14   Bodenaufbau Terrasse   OG

Leimbinder 15x25
                        2,5cm - Lattenrost
                        Holzunterkonstr.
                        3-5cm-Estrich
                        1 Lg PAE-Folie
                        2x6cm - Extrudierte Wärmedämm.
                        3 Lg.Bitum.Isolierung
                        5cm - Gefälle Estrich (mit Frostschutz)
                        18cm - STB Decke   Wohnen

                        Blechkante-Hochzug   +0.30

Wasserspeier
Holzprofil
mit Tropfnase
                        Holzriegelwandaufbau
                        1,9cm-Douglasienplatten-wasserfest/gebürstet/unbechandelt
                        3/5cm-Montagelattung/Hinterlüftung
                          Windbremse
                        16cm-Holzriegelkonstruktion
                        10cm-Wärmedämmung(FDPL)   EG
                          Dampfbremse
                        2,4cm-Vollschalung
                        0,9cm-Birkenplatten-geölt

VERTIKALSCHNITT-TERRASSE/HOLZRIEGELWAND

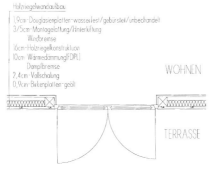

Holzriegelwandaufbau
1,9cm-Douglasienplatten-wasserfest/gebürstet/unbechandelt
3/5cm-Montagelattung/Hinterlüftung
  Windbremse
16cm-Holzriegelkonstruktion
10cm-Wärmedämmung(FDPL)
  Dampfbremse   WOHNEN
2,4cm-Vollschalung
0,9cm-Birkenplatten-geölt

                                          TERRASSE

HORIZONTALSCHNITT-ANSCHLUSS FENSTER/HOLZRIEGELWAND
AUSGANG TERRASSE

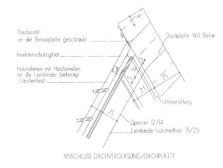

Flachstahl-
an die Betonplatte geschraubt   Dachplatte-WU Beton

Insektenschutzgitter

Holzrahmen mit Holzlamellen
an die Leimbinder befestigt
-Lärchenholz   Hinterlüftung

                        Sparren 12/14
                        Leimbinder-Lärchenholz 15/25

ANSCHLUSS DACHVERGLASUNG/DACHPLATTE

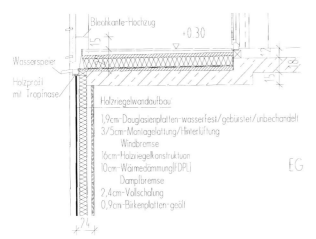

Blechkante-Hochzug   +0.30

Wasserspeier

Holzprofil
mit Tropfnase

Holzriegelwandaufbau
1,9cm-Douglasienplatten-wasserfest/gebürstet/unbechandelt
3/5cm-Montagelattung/Hinterlüftung
  Windbremse   EG
16cm-Holzriegelkonstruktion
10cm-Wärmedämmung(FDPL)
  Dampfbremse
2,4cm-Vollschalung
0,9cm-Birkenplatten-geölt

DACHPLATTE - HORIZONTAL SCHNITT

AUFBAU DACHPLATTE

25cm-Sichtbetondachplatte (B300)
3/5cm Lattung/Hinterlüftung
14cm-FDPL
2,4cm-Sparschalung
Dampfbremse
0,9cm-Birkenplatten

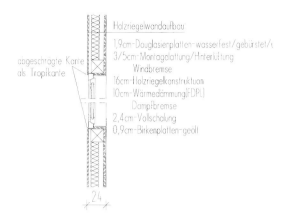

Holzriegelwandaufbau

1,9cm-Douglasierplatten-wasserfest/gebürstet/ι
3/5cm-Montagelattung/Hinterlüftung
   Windbremse
16cm-Holzriegelkonstruktuon
10cm-Wärmedämmung(FDPL)
   Dampfbremse
2,4cm-Vollschalung
0,9cm-Birkenplatten-geölt

abgeschrägte Kante
als Tropfkante

24

Wendell Burnette
Studio residence in sunnyslope
Arizona, USA

The building is located on a small, quarter-acre site in the virgin Sonoran desert in Arizona. Set in a dense neighborhood of the late '50s to early '70s, arid ranch-style houses surround the site along the west face of the Phoenix Mountain Preserve.

Wendell Burnette has built for himself, his wife and his son this house-office in an unfashionable part of town. The design solution is a man-made canyon that renders the surrounding neighborhood less visible; focusing the view and creating a sense of isolation from the desert mountains to the east. An internal court allows natural light to penetrate the 92 foot long bar, providing a moment of focus within the canyon. From the auto and pedestrian entry, the internal garden is the focus, an oasis of light, shade and water, a slot which one climbs up through to reach the separate interior volumes and the outdoor living spaces that lie above and below. This vertical movement culminates in a clear acrylic plunge pool suspended in mid-air by stainless steel cable, rendering the court with   refracted light. The pool is accessed by a sky-bridge that connects the ocean liner like roof terraces with views of sunrise and sunset and the city grid of lights at night.

In the interior, the multifunction zone articulated by the north wall creates symmetrical and asymmetrical relationships with the more numerous north slots. The primary circulation is along the opposite south wall where the sundial effect across the floor originates. Wood is used primarily as a mold and is recycled back into the house as interior finish. All east-west partitions are suspended panels of MDO plywood on an abacus cable system that minimizes overall partition thickness and also allows light to extend across the concrete floor and ceiling. A water-based, non-toxic form release agent was utilized on the kraft paper form surface. This particular agent was selected because it was known to render the formwork a deep reddish-brown color as a natural result of the chemical reaction between the release agent and concrete. Panels were cleaned, edges bonded with Alder and clear sealed with a water based non-toxic product and buffed to a reflective finish (silver with oblique light) similar to hundred year old saddle leather.

All north-south partitions are semi-translucent glass allowing the sunrise and sunset to penetrate the full length of the plan. Privacy is achieved with auto-tint film technology that allowed on-site definition of the extension to be made regarding proportion and privacy while mantaining framed views of the desert site or a particular mountain ridge beyond.

Photographs: Bill Timmerman

An artificial canyon made with masonry walls makes it possible to ignore the otherwise inevitable views of the neighbouring dwellings.

Burnette has used basic materials: masonry, steel, concrete and glass that he has transformed into a subtle and sculptural construction located in the middle of the desert.

Second floor plan

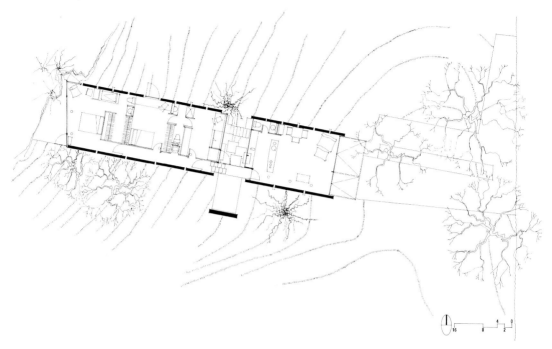

First floor plan

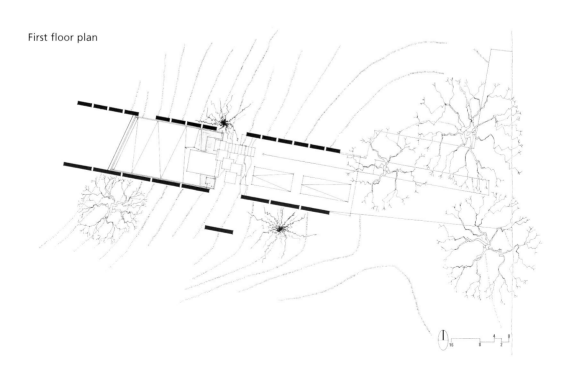

The composition of the south façade necessarily prevents the entrance of sunlight in this desert setting; by contrast, the north façade is completely transparent in order to bring the maximum amount of light into the interior.

Both the pedestrian and vehicle access lead to an inner courtyard that organizes the vertical circulation up to the residential floor.

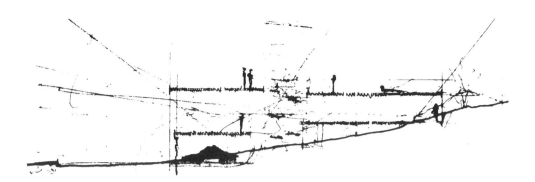

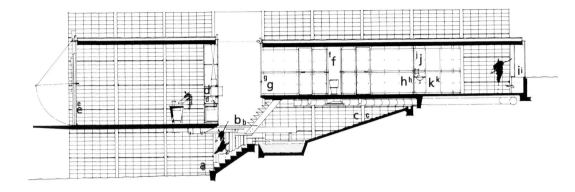

Longitudinal section

a. Carport
b. Entry court
c. Pool
d. Kitchen
e. Livingroom
f. Bathroom
g. Studio
h. Bedroom
i. Master bedroom
j. Master bathroom
k. Dressing

The house's structure consists of two parallel rows of post-stressed masonry walls that support the floor slabs made of concrete laid in situ.

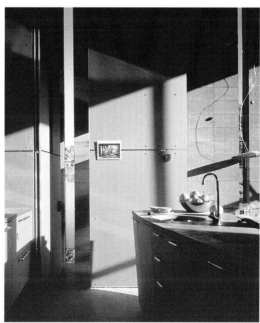

Schmidt, Hammer & Lassen
Thorninghøj Housing Scheme
Kolding, Denmark

The characteristic ring-shaped site plan, which the Thorninghoj housing scheme had to respect, was the result of a site plan competition in 1988. Thorninghoj consists of 65 housing units and a common house, which lies on the summit of the site at a junction of the municipal path system. The housing scheme is divided into four groups with two and three stories.

The units have direct exterior access from a common stairway to the first floor, where there is access to the units via a small stairway, as well as from suspended balcony corridors on the second floor with stairways at distinctive locations.

The buildings are built as large timber structures of oil-treated redwood, which in time will weather to a characteristic silver-grey.

All of the bays are of reddish-yellow, rough surfaced brick. The final color harmony will be achieved when the facades are weathered.

The windows and doors are dark with distinctive ventilation grills in coordinated colors. The windows in the brickwork are painted white. All the buildings have broad roof eaves, which protect the balconies as well as the facades.

Photographs: Jens Nygaard

The buildings that form the housing complex were built using large structures of red sequoia wood treated with special oils for weather-resistance.

Dark tones predominate in the buildings' windows and doors, while the ventilation grills have been painted different colors. All the buildings of the complex have wide eaves that protect the balconies and façades from inclement weather.

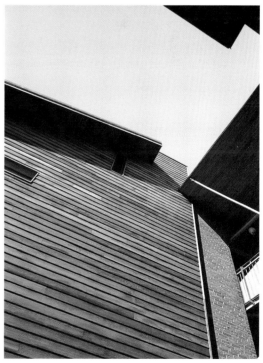

Circus Architects
Vaight apartment
London, UK

The loft has been formed knocking together two shell spaces to provide one substantial double height volume of a scale rarely to be found in central London, where it is located. Carved from the muscular confines of an old printing house, the space comes with thick concrete columns, downstand beams and galvanized steel window frames of industrial scale.

In order to accommodate a family of four, the brief stipulated the inclusion of three bedrooms, three bathrooms, and as much double-height space for the kitchen, dining and family areas as possible. The solution found by the architects involved the piling up of bedrooms as far toward the back of the floor plan as possible, thereby freeing up the wide strip of space facing the street.

This spatial organization provides a bright and open space that allows for an unconventional lifestyle. The kitchen area penetrates into the living and dining area next to a closed free-standing volume, which encloses a small study. The upper level living area overlooks these spaces.

Photographs: Richard Glover

Axonometric projection

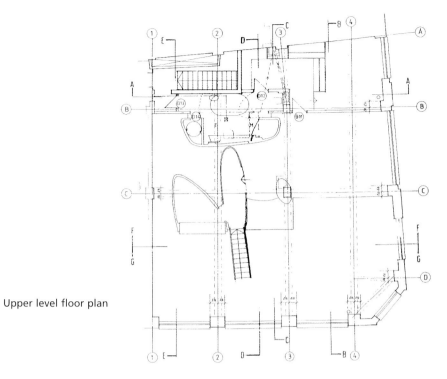

Upper level floor plan

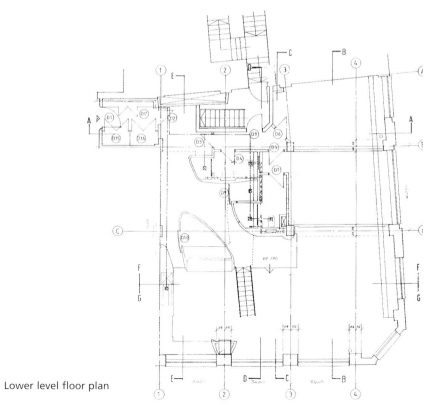

Lower level floor plan

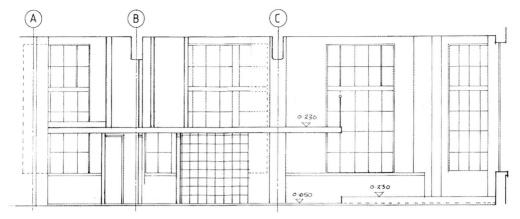

Section CC

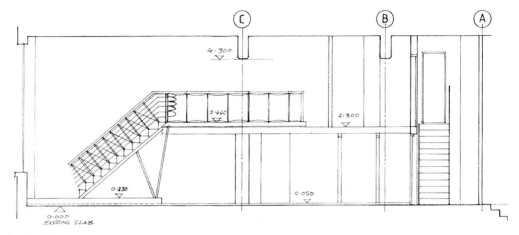

Section DD

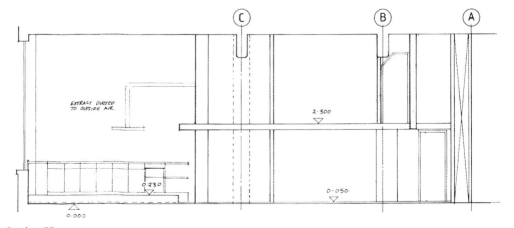

Section EE

Rem Koolhaas
Dutch house
The Netherlands

Marking the termination and final frontier of the ice age, a moraine remains as a Dutch hill, fifty meters above sea level. The 5000 m^2 site is located here, in a forest of pine on a beach of fine golden sand. Aside from the unstable ground conditions, specific site requirements included a height restriction of four meters above the adjacent road and an excessive limitation of buildable area. Literal interpretations of these givens dictated the maximum frame; manipulations of the terrain were subsequent. A drive-through path was carved out to ensure efficiency of access and exit.

The program consists of facilities for two permanent residents –the parents– and for three grown daughters, who visit occasionally. To diminish the fact of their absence, a programmatic split was introduced, materialized by the slab, which is held by one volume while holding the other. The focus of the architects was how to translate two different patterns of occupancy related to specific site conditions as autonomous elements with moments of interaction, and further, how to compress a maximum program into a minimum of formal gestures.

At ground level, one wrapping wall defines a continuity of interior spaces and patios for the daughters' quarters, an introverted and grounded space.

The floating deck supports a crystallized container of the parents' programme. A single hinge –the pivoting bridge/horizontal door– feeds both bedroom units with patio above, service entry below.

The wall itself contains all functional elements, dictating adjacent activity but leaving the surrounding space free within the glass box – physically detached from but visually inclusive of the surrounding landscape. Various treatments of glass and shadings manipulate this relationship according to the program and orientation.

The node of the house is a central ramp providing visual and functional connection between the two counterparts. Paradoxically, this physical cut is where reconciliation is found.

Photographs: Christian Richters

A surface that floats above the land serves as a base for the glazed volume that contains the parents' rooms.

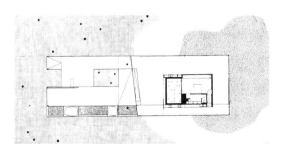

Upper level floor plan

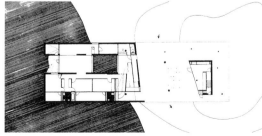

Lower level floor plan

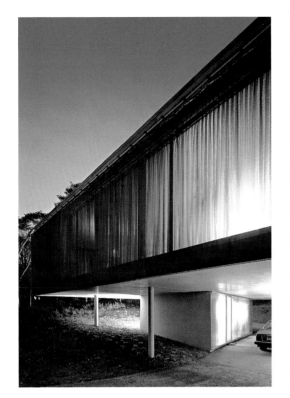

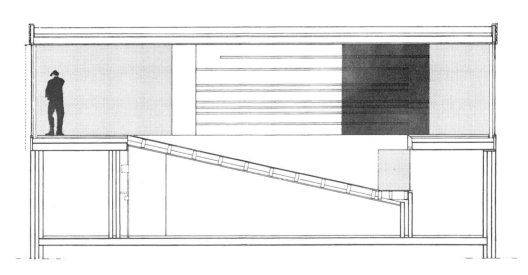

Cross section through the access ramp

The ramp that provides access to the dwelling connects the two parts into which it is divided both physically and visually.

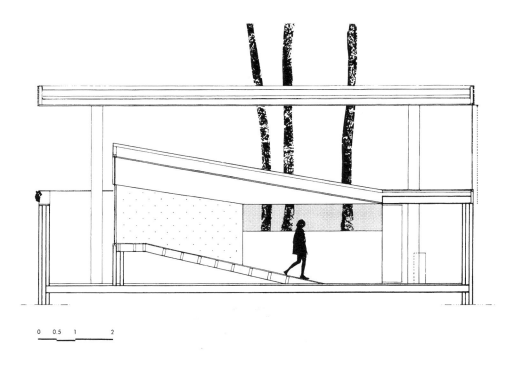

Cross section of the access ramp

Anne Lacaton
& Jean Philippe Vassal

Maison à Lege

Cap Ferret, France

This dwelling is in a wonderful location, directly facing Arcachon Bay and the Atlantic Ocean to the west of Bordeaux. It is a privileged space, one of the last undeveloped plots in an area with magnificent views over the water. Due to the characteristics of the land, an extension of sand dunes whose crest is 15 m above the level of the water, populated by fifty pines rising to 30 m, the architects made an effort to design a building that was able to adapt to and take advantage of its environment. The client brief consisted of building a dwelling on this site without damaging the environment and its qualities. The project maintains the density of the forest (no trees were cut down) and respects the natural rise and fall of the land. Six trees transect the house. On the roof, transparent planes of plastic sheets are tightened to the trunks with flexible rubber. They can glide on the edges of holes in the roof when the trees are moving with the wind.

The house is a platform of 210 m^2 on a single level, built on pillars 2 to 4 meters high according to the slope of the land. This makes it possible to pass under the house and to have better views of the landscape from the interior of the dwelling. The structure is made of steel and the facades are of corrugated aluminum with openings of corrugated transparent fiberglass panels. The lower surface of the floor slab is covered with the same corrugated aluminum, which reflects the light reflected on the water. Finally, the front facade facing Arcachon Bay was left totally transparent, with sliding glass doors.

Photographs: Philippe Ruault

An aluminium spiral staircase leads to the 30 sqm terrace that is at the entrance to this unusual dwelling.

In addition to creating an unusual visual effect, the pines incorporated into the building help to camouflage it in the site.

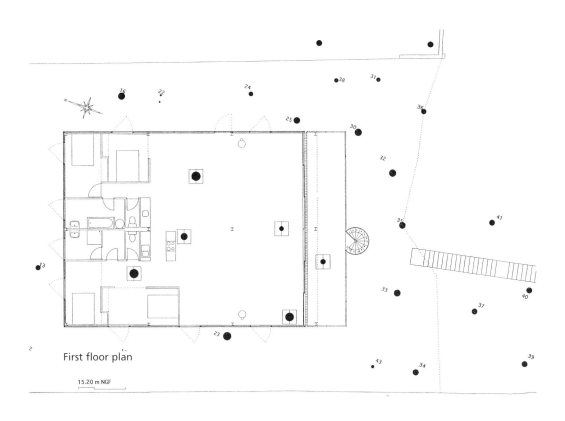

First floor plan

15.20 m NGF

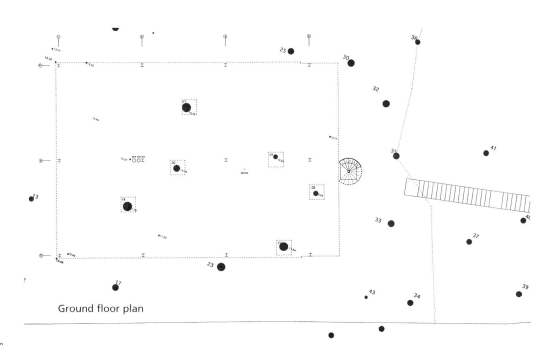

Ground floor plan

South-north longitudinal section

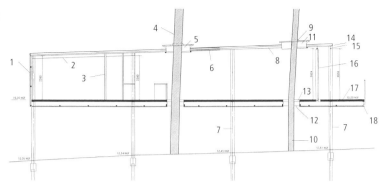

1. Aluminum
2. Plasterboard ceiling
3. Partition with plasterboard
4. Pine trunk
5. Outer ribbing
6. Corrugated aluminum
7. Hea 180
8. Hea 100
9. Steel hoop around the trunk
   + strip of flexible rubber
10. Pine trunk 27
11. Outer ribbing
12. Polyethylene fabric
13. Plywood plaque
14. Drainage strip
15. Galvanized sheet folded into an
    L-shape to protect door and window
    frames
16. Sliding windows on three aluminum
    rails
17. Concrete floor
18. Galvanized steel piece to avoid water
    steepage

Shim & Sutcliffe
Craven Road House
Toronto, Canada

This 1100 ft² urban residence and work space is built on an empty lot on a north-south residential street in Toronto. The client, who was trained as an architect, now works as a researcher/archivist and is also a passionate collector of architectural books and posters. He needed a place to live and work in the city for a construction budget of $CD 100,000. At the outset of the process, he described the numbers of volumes of books, card catalogues and flat files that needed to be accommodated. He also articulated the kind of airy, light-filled room he wanted to work in, as well as the warm, intimate spaces he wished to live in. This project provides a contrast from living space to work space, using simple elements of light, color and ceiling heights.

The project's limited budged was a constraint from the beginning of the design process. The architects worked directly with a selected contractor who reviewed preliminary design proposals and design/development drawings. The owner, contractor and architects all worked collaboratively throughout the design and construction process to ensure that this tight budget could be met. Wood-frame construction, with concrete block basement walls, a concrete basement slab and exterior wood cladding were used. A custom skylight over the stair landing, custom mahogany windows and an exterior custom copper light fixture contrast with the otherwise simple detailing throughout.

This urban project is founded on the belief that cities need to be intensified and densified. This project takes its cues from the existing surroundings. Its front yard setback aligns with its neighbor to the north. Given the 25 foot width of the property, a generous side yard setback on the south side was created, allowing the kitchen/dining area to look onto a future outdoor garden. The building is set back on the north side adjacent to its neighbor. The entrance to the house is located in the middle of the building, reducing the amount of circulation space in the residence and work area. The asymmetrical street, with garages on one side and houses and a sidewalk on the other, has no on-street parking. A simple interlocking paver and grass are used together to provide a front entry court and a space for an occasional visitor to park.

Photographs: Pages 109, 110 and 112: Michael Awad
              Page 113: Robert Hill
              Pages 114 and 115: Steven Evans
              Page 116: James Dow

Site plan

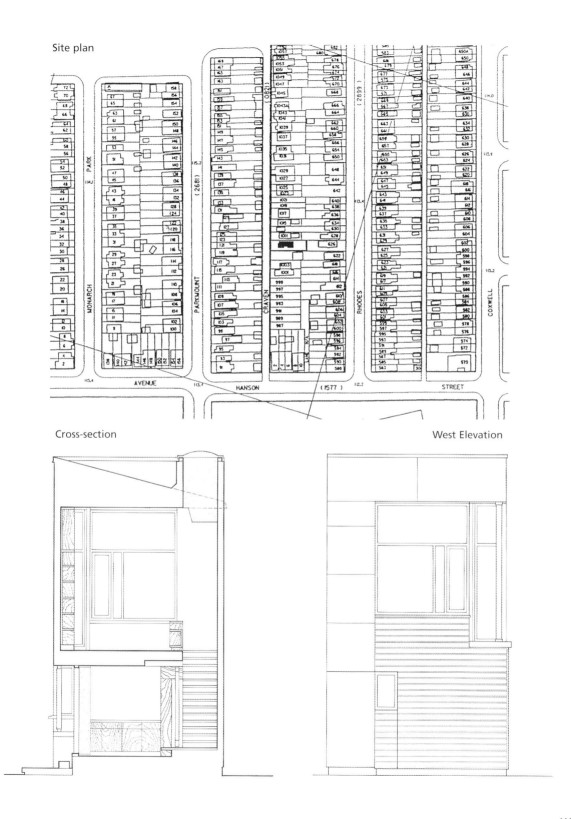

Cross-section

West Elevation

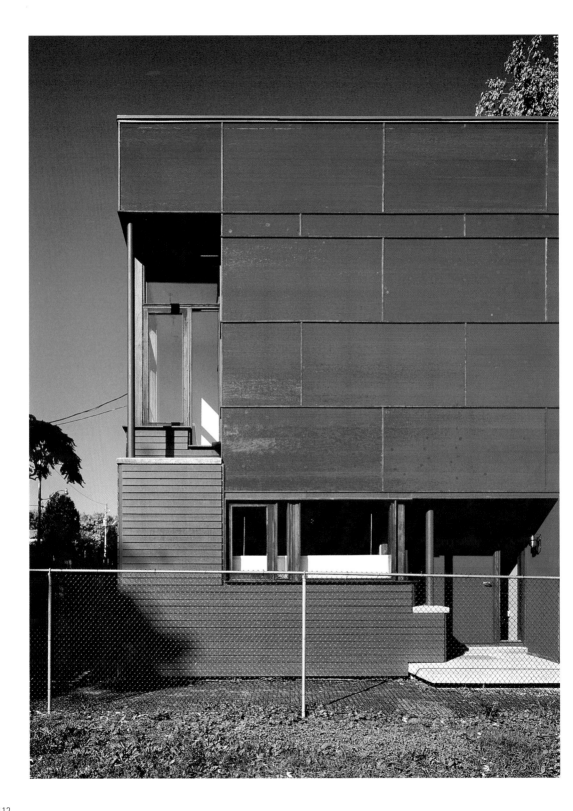

South elevation

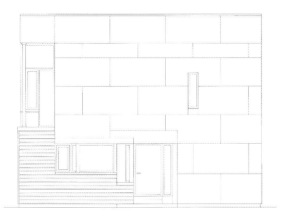

First floor plan

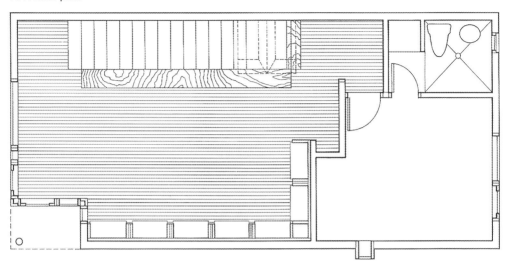

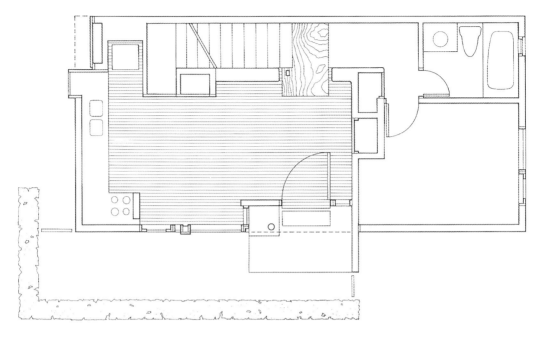

Ground floor plan

As opposed to the cottage-like exterior, the interior more closely resembles an industrial loft, with high ceilings, generous lighting and an open plan. Floor-to-ceiling bookshelves accommodate some of the owner's extensive collection of books and card catalogues.

1   Low-slope asphalt shingles, building paper, 12.7 mm plywood sheeting
2   Wall: 12.7 Douglas fir plywood façade cladding, vertical battens, waterproofing layer on plywood sheeting, glass-fiber insulation, 51/152 mm timber studs, plastic sheet vapor barrier, plasterboard
3   Fixed glazing
4   Maple flooring strips
5   25/102 mm softwood façade boarding
6   76/76/3 mm steel corner angle
7   19/19 mm timber corner bead
8   Vertical cover strip over panel joint
9   Horizontal cover strip over panel joint

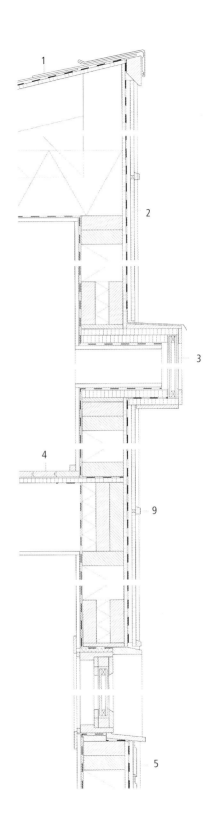

Detail sections

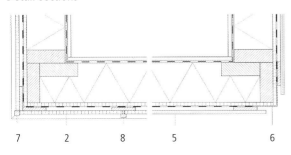

Thom Maine / Morphosis
Blades Residence
Santa Barbara, USA

In June 1990 several hundred homes in the coastal hills of Santa Barbara were destroyed by fire. The clients decided to reframe this catastrophic experience as a catalyst to reinvent their day-to-day existence. Unlike their neighbors who took more "conventional" approaches, they decided to build a house "like nothing they had ever seen before".

The fire left a charred landscape with a gentle sloping grade, several boulders and a cluster of native oaks. Given its suburban/rural context, the introspective strategy of an enclosed project was explored.

Due to the very modest budget, design and craftsmanship were given priority over expensive materials from the very first moment.

The 3800 ft^2 interior spaces are organized as three main spaces adjacent to five smaller exterior rooms, each one a linear sequence of overlapping zones in which the boundaries of public and private spaces are intentionally blurred. Interior light is modulated through subtle openings and recesses that create a sculpted space. The couple shares a very open bedroom, yet each has their individual studios at opposite ends of the house. The upper story studio has expansive views from a corner window that has been carved out as well as an exterior catwalk. The ground floor studio/gallery is a separate wing with clerestory windows and no exterior views.

Photographs: Kim Zwarts

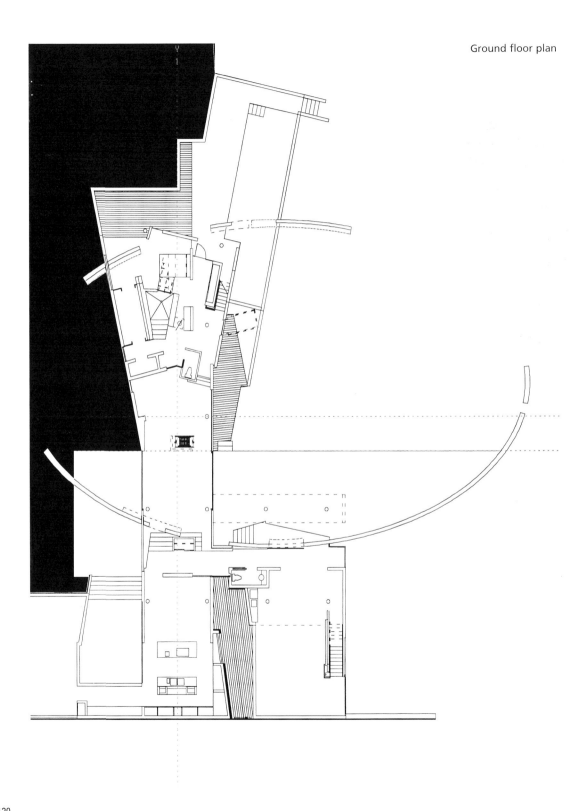

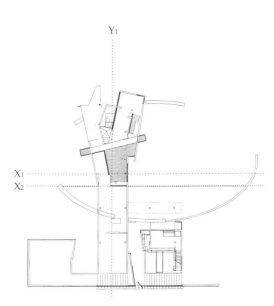

The internal and external volumes of the building overlap, forming a projection over the swimming pool.

The house is organized as three main spaces, each one a linear sequence of overlapping zones in which the boundaries of public and private spaces are intentionally blurred. Interior light is modulated through subtle openings and recesses that create a sculpted space.

Cross sections

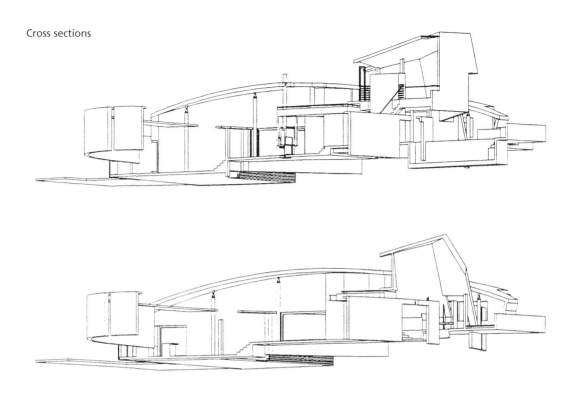

Longitudinal section

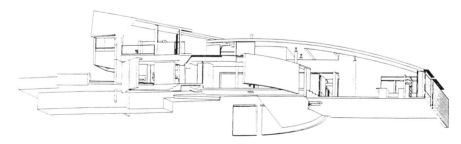

The interior of the dwelling is organized as a large bright, mostly uninterrupted, single space.

Hiroyuki Arima
House in Dazaifu
Dazaifu, Japan

The design scheme behind this house is a device for providing natural views and bringing more light into daily life. It is composed of the combination of certain spaces arising as a result of a study of possible views, light and wind. Life thus follows the order of spaces determined in relation to the exterior. This residence therefore has a standard of value which is different from today's ordinary Japanese residence, standing much closer to the classic conception of a home.

The residence is located not too far from the approach to Dazaifu Shrine. The ground here is uneven, and native bamboo groves and broadleaf trees provide pleasing views with the changing seasons. Two boxes are placed on the slope at a difference in level of 10 meters, facing the hills of Dazaifu. Each one is completely independent at its elevation. The role of the lower box is to cut off the distant views horizontally and to expose the various changes of nature to the interior. Here, the views play an essential part in composing spaces as an element. The interior spaces have no concept of a room, with the "box" forming a large room by itself. In it, the smaller boxes contain functional elements and are placed in an orderly manner. The upper volume also reveals functional elements of the interior.

The upper box opens only vertically, and its role is to separate the interior from the exterior. It consists of two spaces, a light garden with a shallow pool of water, and beyond that Gallery 2. In this space, the resident can vary the influx of light by changing operable partitions. If necessary, the interior can be completely separated from the exterior. The visual relationship between occupant and nature in the upper volume is thus purer than in the lower volume.

The two boxes are connected by a natural path following the slope of the terrain. To live by coming and going between the two volumes means that a part of nature is naturally inserted into the living space.

Photographs: Koji Okamoto

Site plan

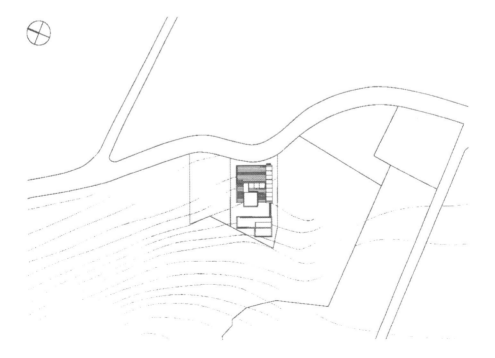

Ground floor plan

A vertical incision in the main volume of the dwelling
provides natural lighting.

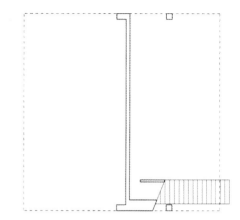

First floor plan

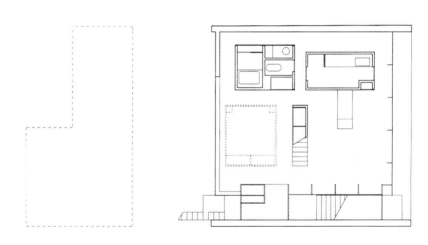

Second floor plan

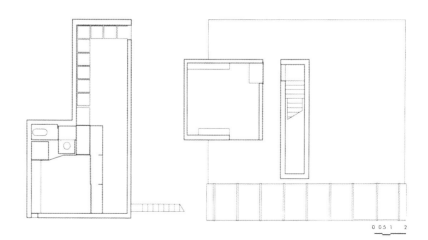

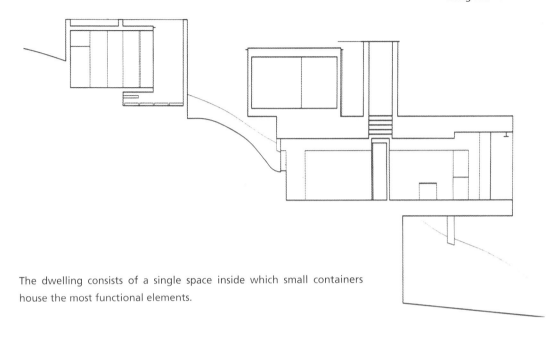

The dwelling consists of a single space inside which small containers house the most functional elements.

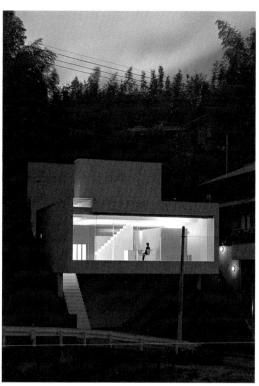

Axonometric projection

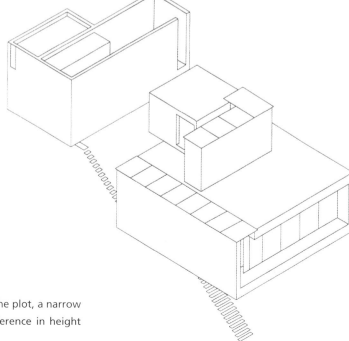

Due to the difficult topography of the plot, a narrow stairway bridges the ten-meter difference in height between the two volumes.

Patrick Hernandez
Pavillon de Garde
Arsac, France

The residence for the custodian of Arsac Castle, in the heart of the Médoc, is located in the castle's entrance driveway. It is a much more radical proposal than that ordinarily seen in individual dwellings as it is closed off to its immediate surroundings, yet open to the sky.

Parked delivery cars can be glimpsed to the north in front of the castle, while a major road lies to the east and, to the south and west, the gaze slides unobstructed over a sprawling expanse of grass. The lack of scenic value in this desert-like environment gave the architect the idea of constructing a veritable oasis, a self-sufficient unit, able to find its own identity, which would fold in on itself. An affirmation of its introversion, blind walls are this structure's response to the immensity of its surroundings. The vertical views through the roof, in turn, respond to this horizontal immensity. In fact, this oasis precisely defines its own boundaries on the surrounding land: the walls of Douglas pine reach the gate, defining the border of the wine-growing domain on one side and, on the other, the exterior private space. A small patio with a sliding door lets additional light into the dwelling from the side. The entire residence –kitchen, sitting room, dining room and bedrooms– benefits from the natural light provided by the glass ceiling. The steel-framed glass structure is part of the attempt to adapt the living space to the industrialized systems used in the construction of greenhouses, a method which this architect had previously used in a restaurant near Bordeaux.

In this type of construction, which gives precedence to vertical views, the garden does not encircle the dwelling, but rather is placed on top of it. The metal wall support structure is extended beyod the roof and forms a pergola designed to hold plants and flowers.

Photographs: Vincent Monthiers

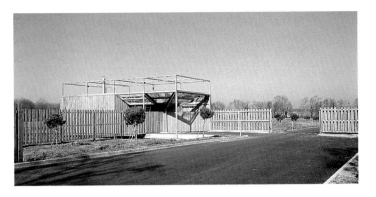

The guardhouse of the castle of Arsac is set in barren surrounding, isolated in a location of such unexciting qualities that the architect made the radical decision to eliminate all side views and to reinforce a large opening toward the open sky by means of a glass roof.

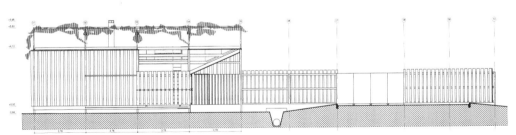

South elevation

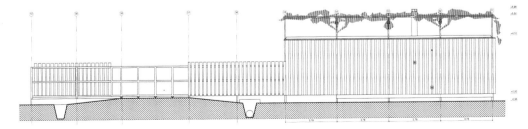

North elevation

East elevation

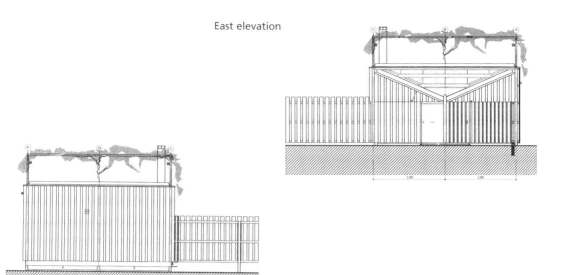

West elevation

143

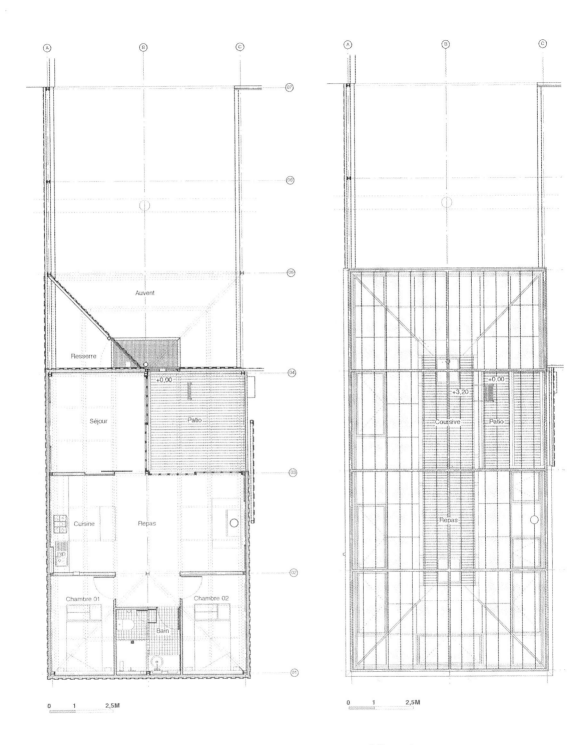

Floor plan

Roof floor plan

The roof is composed of two oblique dou-
ble-glazed panels that rest on a longitudi-
nally centered beam of galvanized steel
that also acts as a gutter.

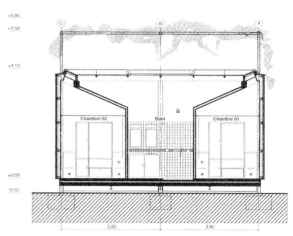

Section 1-1'

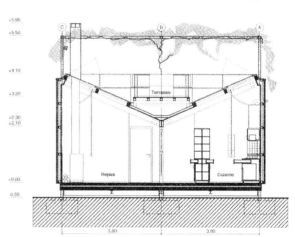

Section 2-2'

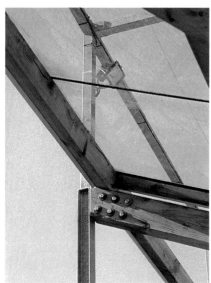

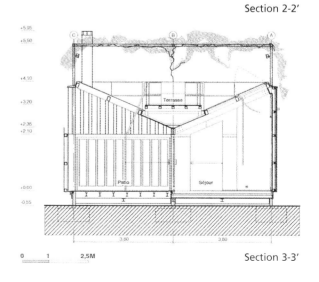

0   1   2,5M

Section 3-3'

The residence has an authentic suspended garden, with a railed terrace that rests above the gutter beam and can be accessed from the court by a folding metal staircase.

Section A-A'

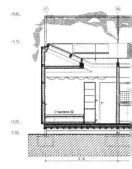

Section B-B'

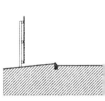

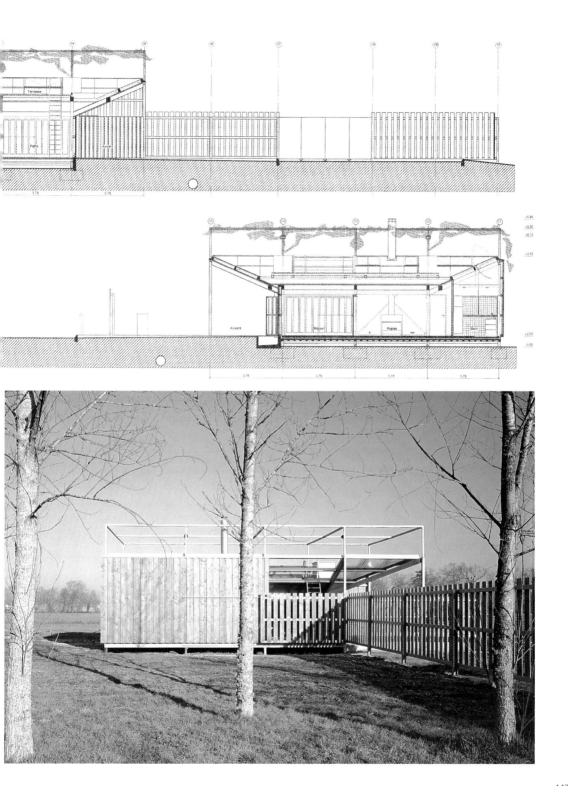

Eugene Tsui
Ecological house of the future
Bao An, Shenzhen, People's Republic of China

This 200 m² apartment is a glimpse of the future of ecological apartment environments in China. The general ambiance is one of living in a natural setting surrounded by the curving and undulating forms of natural wind-swept stone interspersed with moving waterfalls, waterponds and abundant plants. But there is much more than meets the eye. The environment sustains itself with minimum maintenance. It is a living, interconnected system of self-regulating sewage treatment, clean water and air recycling, natural breeze control and self-activating windows that automatically adjust the amount of entering sunlight.

Exterior photovoltaic solar panels convert sunlight into electricity, which is stored for home used. Roof windmills also convert wind to direct power for electrical home use.

In sum, the future ecological house of China will be a place as beautiful and spiritually powerful as the forests, mountains, lakes, deserts and oceans. It is a place where nature and humanity come together for the benefit of both; a rejuvenating place where a person can come closer to the technological wisdom and poetic power of nature. A home of robust physical health, comfort and creative inspiration.

Photographs: Dr. Eugene Tsui

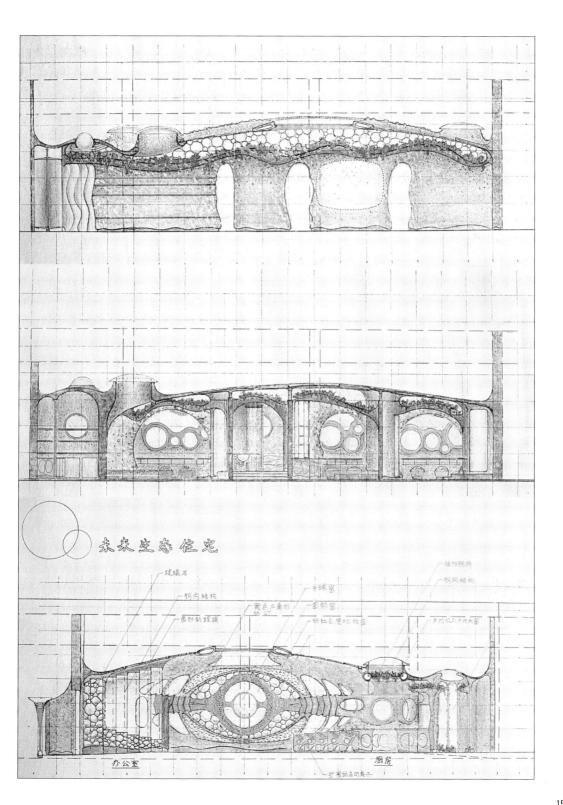

未来生态住宅

玻璃石
钢内结构
圆形的玻璃
黄色三角形的灯
半球窗
圆的窗
粉红色质地的墙
植物张网
钢网结构
黑内机制片状大窗

办公室   厨房

扩宽的白的柱子

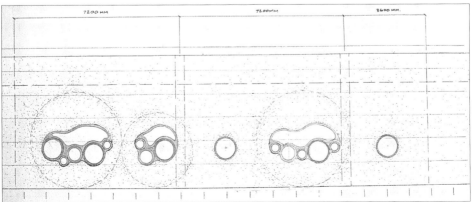

All windows allow viewers to see the left and right of the building's exterior and economically provide greater sunlight and wind resistance.

Christian Drevet
Une maison a Rillieux-la-Pape

Rillieux-la-Pape, France

The body of the building is composed of a heavy, compact box-like volume of exposed concrete that is contained within another, more subtle and lightweight box of steel, wood and glass. The interior volume provides the necessary intimacy for the family's living area; while the work spaces (the stable and granary) and reception area have been inserted into the exterior wrapping.

The entire grouping of volumes is capped by an expansive, fragmented roof with a zigzagging form that juts out over the perimeter of the façade to provide a protective cover for the farm equipment and vehicles. The lightweight, inner box is an open space with divisions drawn by a 1.50x2.50 meter metal framework that supports the roof. This structure is joined to the concrete body, thereby granting it the necessary stability. The windows are composed of wooden boards and framework in the same dimensions.

The entirely glazed south facade, which is shared by both volumes, projects all of the dwelling's spaces toward the vast landscape. Viewed from the access route the copper color of the windowless wood façades restores privacy to the home. The random positioning of interior curtains, sliding windows and exterior awnings throughout the day, along with seasonal changes and occupant use, suggest a lively architecture with a variety of perspectives. Independent of all formal intention, the house reacts to light and heat like a natural element, forming an integral part of the overall landscape.

Photographs: G. Aymard

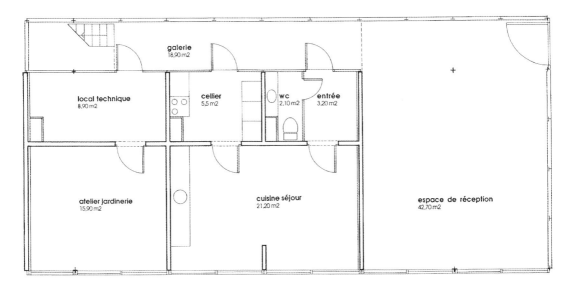

galerie
18,90 m2

local technique
8,90 m2

cellier
5,5 m2

wc
2,10 m2

entrée
3,20 m2

atelier jardinerie
15,90 m2

cuisine séjour
21,20 m2

espace de réception
42,70 m2

Ground floor plan

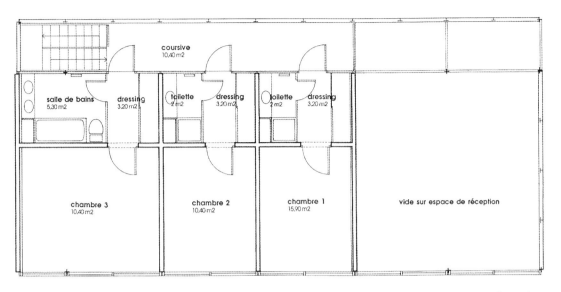

coursive
10,40 m2

salle de bains
5,30 m2

dressing
3,20 m2

toilette
2 m2

dressing
3,20 m2

toilette
2 m2

dressing
3,20 m2

chambre 3
10,40 m2

chambre 2
10,40 m2

chambre 1
15,90 m2

vide sur espace de réception

First floor plan

Cross section

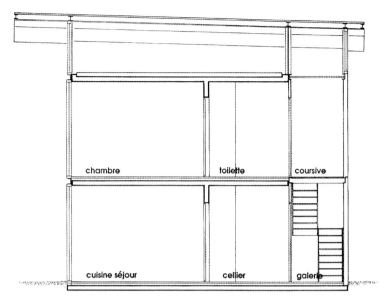

chambre	toilette	coursive
cuisine séjour	cellier	galerie

The body of the building is composed of a heavy, compact box-like volume of exposed concrete that is contained within another, more subtle and lightweight box of steel, wood and glass.

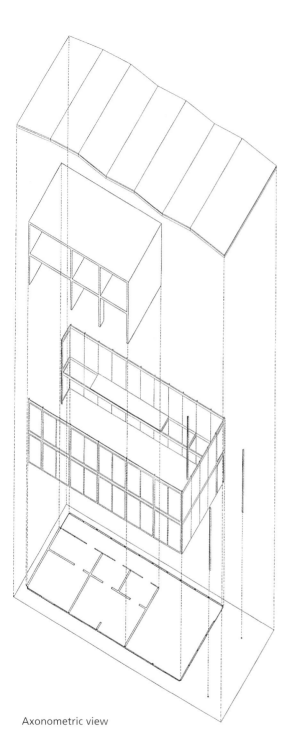

Axonometric view

The random positioning of interior curtains, sliding windows and exterior awnings throughout the day suggest a lively architecture with a variety of perspectives.

Jakob + Macfarlane
Maison t
La Garenne-Colombes, France

After an initial project in 1994, which involved the renovation of an existing house in the suburbs of Paris, a second project was undertaken in order to add a new floor onto the house, creating a 40m^2 loft space for the children.

The architects —who are also the owners of the home— decided to emphasize the new loft by creating a visually distinct identity; and since the occupants of the added space were children, they created a whimsical and fun design scheme in which two separate yet interconnected "playhouses" were created, perched on the roof of the existing house.

The completed project is an enclosing envelope of zinc, broken up into several volumes with the lines of the roof pitched at seemingly random angles. The cold, industrial look of natural zinc is contrasted in the interior by the warmth of lightly varnished fir wood and white-painted planes.

The nooks and hideaways created by sloping angles and non-uniform lines achieves the goal of turning a single loft into two distinct spaces.

At the same time, the dictates imposed by a large number of views have been taken into account. The dovetailing of the volumes thus creates a series of openings with complex geometric forms, offering a variety of views toward the exterior — some skyward, others outward, toward the surrounding neighborhood.

Photographs: Nicolas Borel

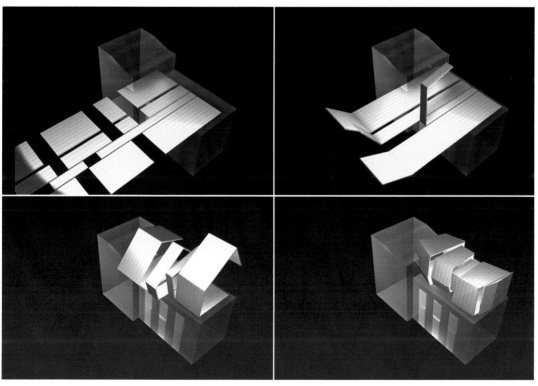

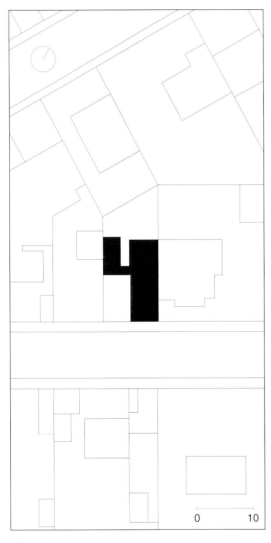

Site plan

0   10

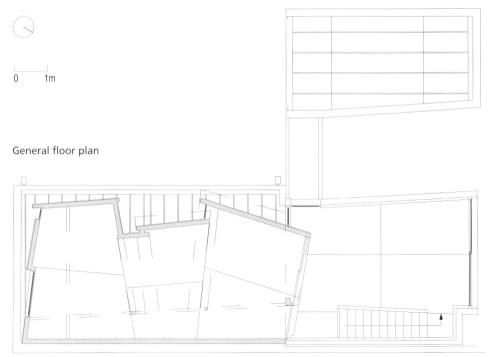

0   1m

General floor plan

The outer shell of the new loft is done entirely in natural zinc, an industrial material contrasted in the interior by the warmth of fir wood and smooth, white walls.

The dovetailing of the volumes creates a series of openings with complex geometric forms, offering a variety of views toward the exterior — some skyward, others outward, toward the street.

LOG ID
Residential Building in the Black Forest
Schramberg, Germany

This home for a family of four is situated on a sloping plot, close to a preexisting detached house in Schamberg, in the Black Forest, overlooking the town and the castle. The architects' aim was to build a solar house, including a separate apartment, which would complement the neighboring house.

Access from the street above is over a footbridge in metal grating alongside the parking platform, which juts out over the garden.

Solar architecture was a basic premise of the new building from the design stage, and is clearly discernible in the ground plan. The body of the construction, with outer walls in 36.5 cm thick Poroton, is compact in order to minimize its surface area and to improve the resulting diffusion of heat.

Solar energy is collected passively in the 64-square-meter glasshouse, which faces southwest and is shaped to take full advantage of the sun as it crosses the sky. The heat thus generated is then used actively, being distributed throughout the 360 square meters of living space.

The plants in the glasshouse also contribute to the health of the family by producing oxygen and absorbing harmful substances.

Daylight enters throug the glasshouse and also through a fanlight in the main body of the house. Beneath the fanlight, a glass reticular arrangement allows natural light to penetrate as far as the living room.

The glasshouse has a steel structure with thermal glass surfaces, while the interiors are in white mineral plaster for the walls and white marble for the floors.

The project is a successful example of how to combine environmentalism and high-quality detached housing.

Photographs: Reiner Blunck

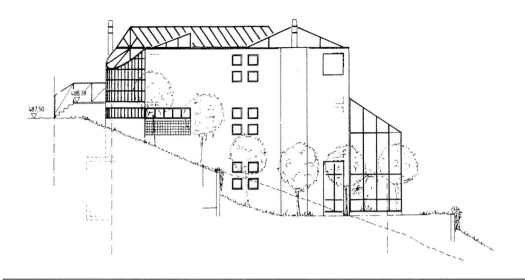

Light is diffused through the glass surfaces, creating a transparent space in which reflections are reinforced by the highly polished floor and the depth produced by the glass-floored landing above.

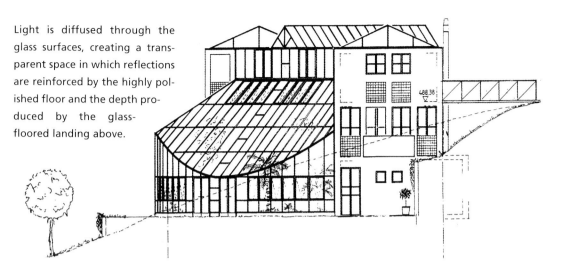

Ground floor plan

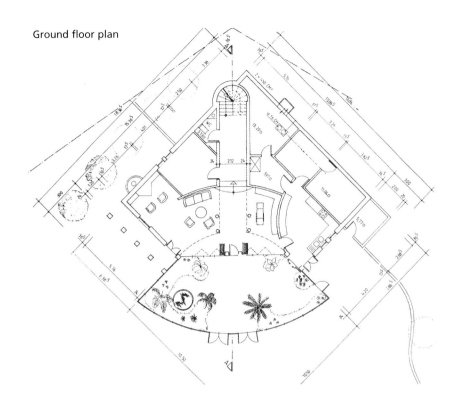

First floor plan

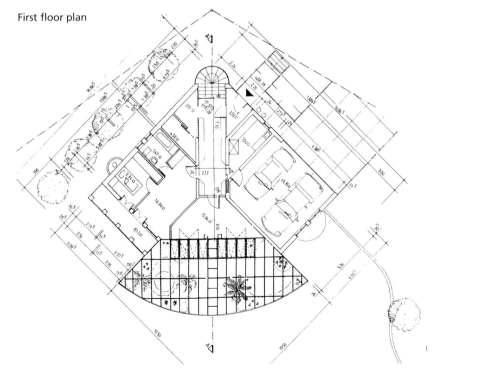

Second floor plan

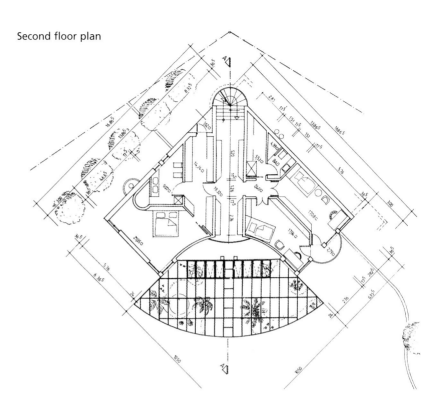

Roof floor plan

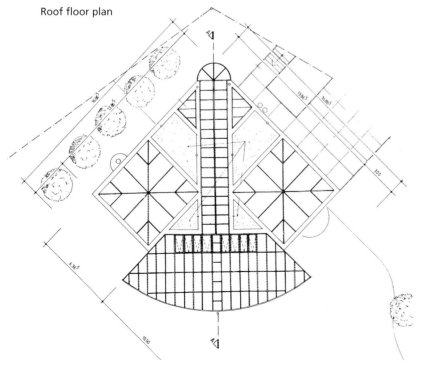

Behnisch & Partners
Charlotte house
Sillenbuch, Germany

The Charlotte house is almost an exception in the work of Behnisch & Partners, whose projects are normally of a greater scope. However, in the design of this dwelling, they show a great knowledge of the architectural models of the past, and great acuity in adapting them to the functional and environmental needs of the present. Indeed, the difficult problem facing them in this suburb of Stuttgart, with very high land prices, is similar to that faced by Adolf Loos in the design of the Horner house in Vienna (1913): a very small plot on which the planning regulations drastically reduced the permitted ground plan.

In addition to the main dwellinfg, the program was to include several rented apartments, although due to the planning regulations and the size of the plot only one was left in the final design.

It was located on the top level in order to provide intimacy and privacy for the different families that would live in the buildings. The functional requirements called for the installation of an elevator, and all the rooms had to have certain dimensions and receive a special treatment.

The most outstanding feature of the design is the vaulted roof, which provides a large habitable space and differentiates the building from its typological environmet of dwellings with peaked roofs.

The house introduces radical innovations in its adaptation to the environmental requirements. The ecological intent of the deisgn is seen both in the construction systems and in the selection of materials: paints and lacquers made from natural resins, wood that is not protected by chemical products, cellulose-based recyclable materials as an alternative to the habitual mineral fiber insulations and so forth.

In the design of the smaller facades we can also see this attention to ecology and the environment: the south facade is open towards the street in order to take advantage of the light and solar energy, whereas the north facade is more closed to save energy and ensure privacy.

Photographs: Behnisch & Partners, Christian Kandzia

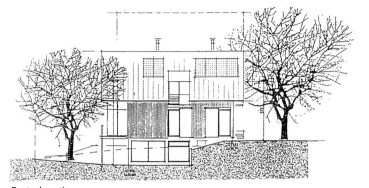

East elevation

First floor plan

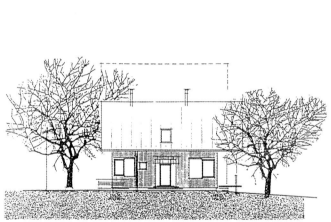

West elevation

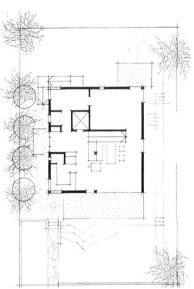

Ground floor plan

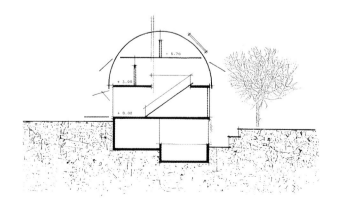

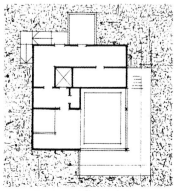

Basement floor plan

The plans, the section and the facades reveal the architectural solution to the problem of the small ground plan permitted by the planning regulations. It consists of a very compact and almost cube-like volume (from basement to attic) that takes advantage of the sloping land to locate a semi-basement. The roof, which brings to mind a covered wagon, houses an apartment. The metal roof cladding bears a battery of solar panels.

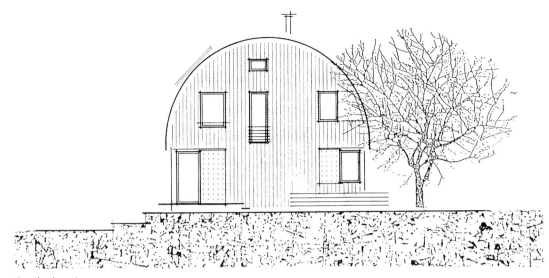

South elevation

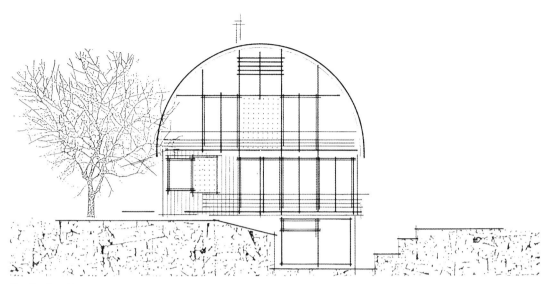

North elevation

Love-Architecture & Urbanism
Softech home; Solar house
Gamlitz, Styria. Austria

This is the prototype of a system house intended for mass production. Softech, a specialist in low-energy construction, launched the idea of developing a system house combining the highest aesthetic standards with current low-energy techniques.

The house was conceived as a "summer/winter-house": the living room (winter-living room) corresponds in size with the terrace (summer-living room). Both are connected by a large sliding glass-wall. Bathroom and kitchen can be used equally from the summer and winter living room. This concept enlargens the house beyond its built surface.

The usefulness of the house was extended in the summer by creating a protected terrace in front of the living room and by then connecting the two via a large sliding and revolving door.

The rooms were also optimized in regard to their use and minimized corridors and service spaces.

Developing the construction system, the following requirements were given priority. First was the combination of the advantages of massive construction (heat storage, acoustic protection) with the advantages of lightweight walls (no drying time, good heat insulation, quick regulation of room temperature). The second demand was the employment of natural, regenerating materials, using local wood.

The outer walls were constructed with non-treated, glued larch boards, cellulose insulation and natural gypsum fiberboards.

The estimated time for building this dwelling was 6 to 8 months, a very short time bearing in mind the quality of the finishes and its floor space of 156 m^2.

Photographs: Andress Balloon, Love-Architecture & Urbanism

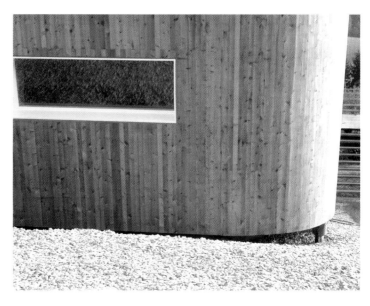

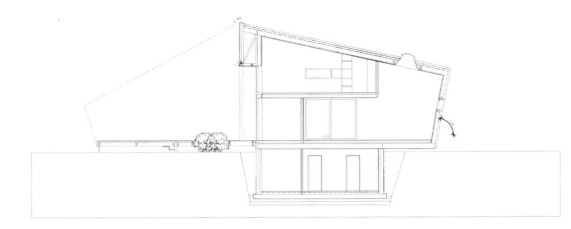

This solar house is the largest of a series of dwellings made in conjunction with Softech, a company specializing in research and development of renewable energy systems applied to construction. The spaces were configured so that the dwelling could be used equally in summer and in winter.

In the design of the construction system it was decided to combine the advantages of a solid construction (heat storage, acoustic protection) with the advantages of light walls (no desiccating, good thermal insulation, rapid regulation of the temperature of rooms). All wood used is local, and the other materials are also natural and recyclable.

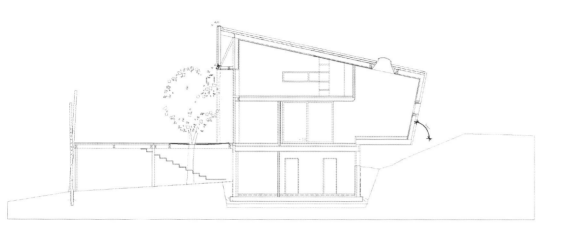

Cross sections

Floor plans

Upper floor plan

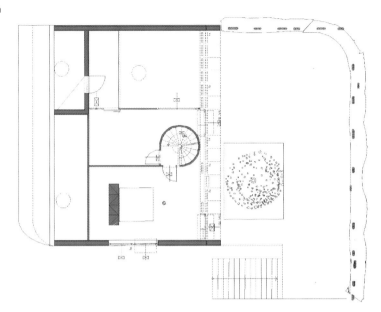

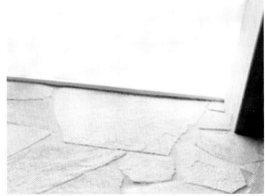

Lower floor plan

Mario Botta
House in Montagnola
Montognola, Switzerland

The architecture of Mario Botta is characterized by its formal power and the strong presence of its volumes. His buildings do not attempt to blend into their surroundings; rather, they aim to impose themselves on them, to implant themselves with all the vigour of their architectural mass and become landmarks in the landscape. This single-family dwelling is a clear example of this tendency. Located in the Swiss canton of Ticino, it is not subordinated to its Alpine setting. Instead, it takes advantage of the relief of the setting to emerge with force from the site, seeking to make a plastic, expressive impact.

This project bases its formal strength on volume. The building rises out of the ground to form a large semicylindrical body.

The curve of the outer wall is interrupted by a large glazed area which is set back from the principal plane. These windows flood the house with light and open it up to views of the valley. A row of bull's-eyes along the top introduce a nautical idiom into the Alpine context.

A longitudinal body housing the leisure facilities (swimming pools, sauna and gym) and a large garage was attached to the main volume, taking advantage of the slope.

Photographs: Pino Musi

Site plan

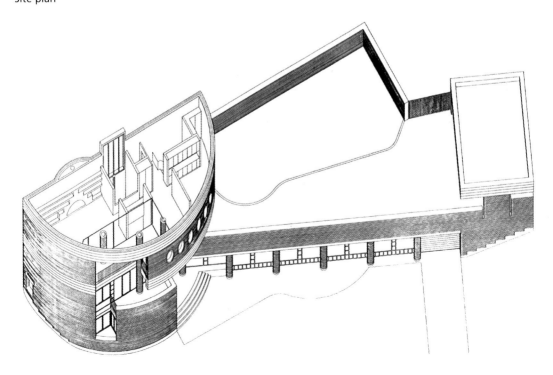

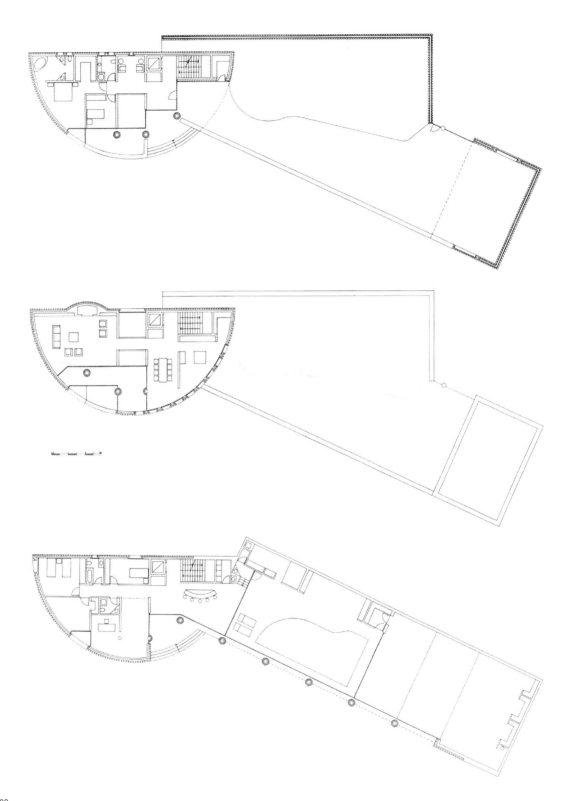

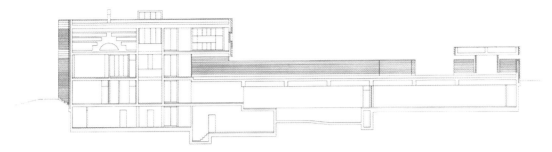

Longitudinal section

The house in Montagnola is forcefully set into the landscape as a large semi-cylindrical volume from which there emerges a longitudinal body housing the recreational installations at the point where the two main volumes meet. The row of bull's-eyes introduce an unprecedented idiom into these Alpine surroundings,

Studio Archea
House in Costa San Giorgo
Florence, Italy

This apartment is located in an old medieval tower near Ponte Vecchio, in the heart of Florence. The original Renaissance building had large wooden beams that gave it a certain majesty, and the challenge consisted in designing a residential space that took advantage of the exceptional characteristics of the Quattrocento structure to create a functional and contemporary atmosphere.

The space is designed around a curvilinear stone wall that organizes the diverse functions of the dwelling and supports the metal beams of the mezzanine, which is used as the night area. This wall acts as a bookcase, leaves the kitchen semi-concealed, houses in its perimeter the stairwell, and divides the spaces so that the materials define and organize the different atmospheres of the dwelling. An iron staircase set against the opposite wall leads to a platform giving access to the mezzanine. From this horizontal platform, a walkway also leads to a small pool over the dining room with a bathroom next to it. This area of the upper floor is in the new stone part of the apartment; the rectilinear mezzanine is separated by a small wooden floor space.

Because of the small size of the scheme, the architects were able to design all the elements in detail, avoiding prefabrication and creating unique, almost sculptural objects.

The architects showed great respect for tradition in the use of natural stone, in the conservation of the original ceiling and in the distribution of the furniture.

A single space and different atmospheres for one person: this is the result of this intervention in a building infused with history.

Photographs: Alessandro Ciampi

The void created between the two main volumes is used as a corridor on the ground floor. On the upper floor, this free space offers different views and perspectives, and opens up the dimensions of the apartment.

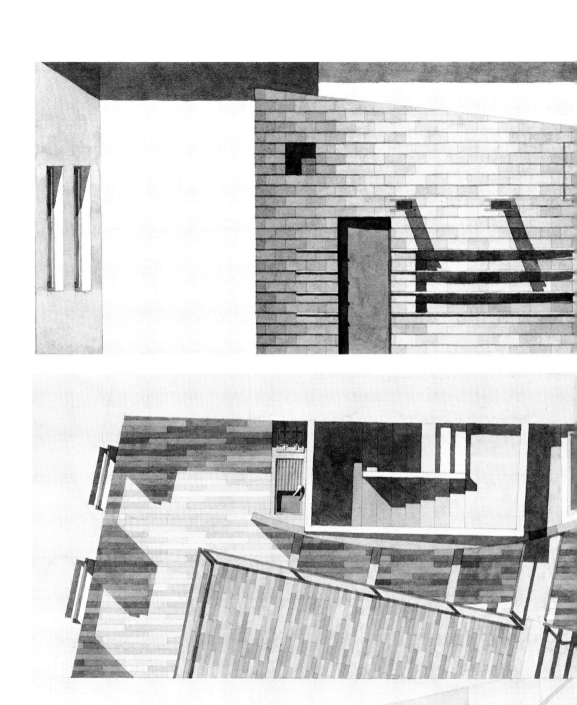

Julia B. Bolles & Peter L. Wilson
House Hub

Münster, Germany

This small addition to a 1960's Modernist atrium house respects the language of the object in which it is found.

The team of architects Julia Bolles and Peter Wilson have made a careful and exquisite rehabilitation, based, as they declare, on the "fascination for clarity, optimism and simple geometries of the last days of functionalism". The structure of the original house is transcended through the insertion of a new vertical element, a volume clad in an intense blue brick that faces the internal court. This foreign object, that emphasizes and puts energy into the geometry of the complex, breaks through the artificial horizon of the existing flat roof.

Brought about by the needs of new use requirements (a larger living space, a small studio) the additions are reduced to five discrete elements: the blue glazed brick wall, the zinc wall, the sun louvers (a new horizontal factor), the internal swing wall and, as a nexus for the whole composition, the central fireplace.

Photographs: Christian Richters

Ground floor plan

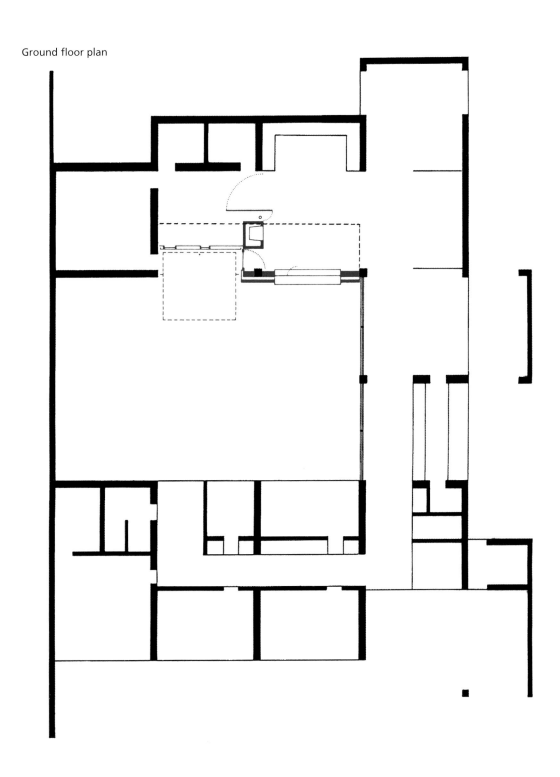

Sketches before and after the intervention

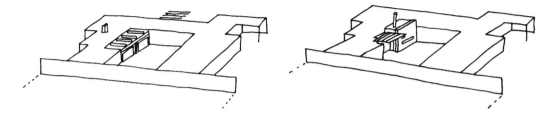

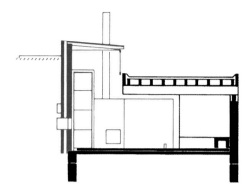 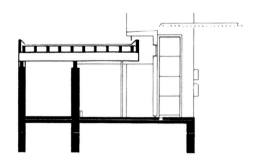

Cross section

The new fireplace, situated in a central position, acts as a link between the existing building and the elements that form the new intervention.

North elevation

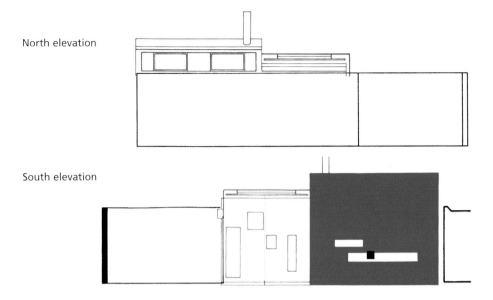

South elevation

The project aims to solve the existing building's problems of space by providing sufficient floor area to extend the living-room and create a small studio.

Silvia Gmür & Livio Vacchini
3 Single–Family Houses
Beinwil am See, Argovia. Switzerland

Located in the Swiss town of Beinwil am see these three single-family modules stand out from the architecture of the area due to their special design and arrangement. Three identical dwellings located on a hillside with a view of the lake give form to a single complex. The different modules share their foundations in a kind of pedestal that determines part of their architectural character, enhancing their role in the landscape.

The dwellings create a compositional rhythm in which the predominant geometry of the floors is the square, whereas in the elevations it is the rectangle. This rhythm is determined by a linear succession of "solids" and "voids" in which the former act as private spaces while the latter are used for the common living areas. The private space is divided in turn into porch and room, so the differentiation between exterior and interior is slightly blurred. The facades are composed of three differentiated elements that are used for their functionality and their aesthetic qualities: cement, glass and "air" that in the void is converted into matter. It is an architecture that tends towards the essential without expressive rhetoric or metaphoric language, an architecture without superfluous details in which the orientation becomes crucial through its form, structures and materials.

The generous use of natural light, a perfect organization of the spaces, the choice of specific materials, and the careful orientation of the structures are the basic ingredients of this work full of order and balance. These three dwellings not only produce multiplicity, variety, potentiality and virtuality, but also a way of inhabiting and combining private and common spaces.

Photographs: Vaclav Sedy

Ground floor plan

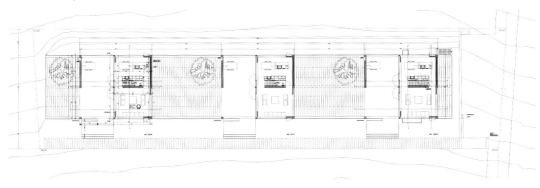

The elementary rhythm of the square-cube is added to the horizontal nature of the base on which the three dwellings are placed, creating an expressive and symphonic effect in which the different dimensions seem to mediate between the vertical and the horizontal, and between the solid and the void.

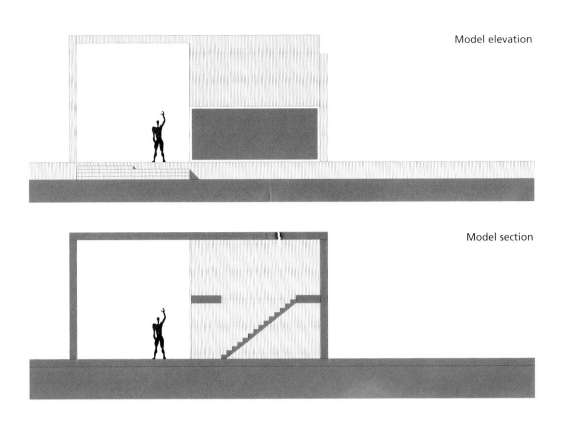

Model elevation

Model section

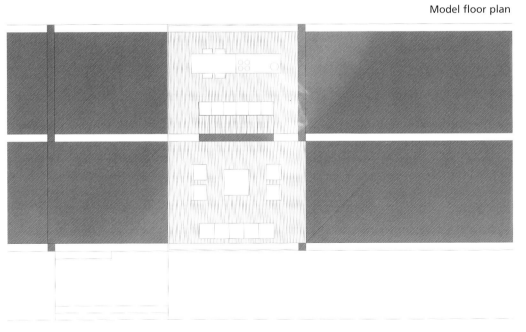

Model floor plan

North-east elevation

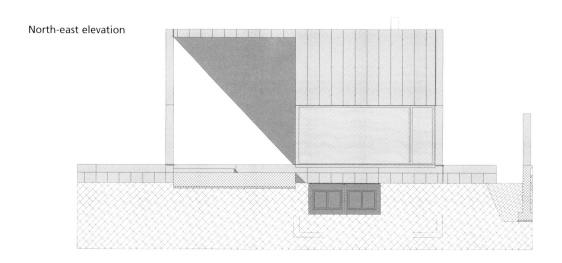

South-west elevation

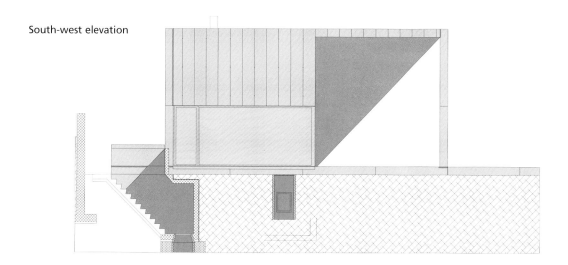

South-east elevation

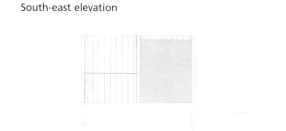

North-west elevation

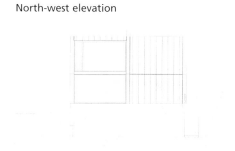

First floor plan

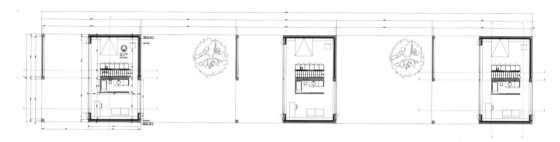

In the interior, the three dwellings have the same simple and functional layout. The kitchen-dining room and living room are located on the ground floor, while on the upper floor a large bedroom occupies the entire ground space, with the exception of a central module housing a bathroom, a fitted cupboard and the stairwell.

Richard Meier
Rachofksy House
Dallas, USA

Set in a suburban landscape, this house/private museum is anchored to the ground by a podium clad in black granite that extends both in front of and behind the main body of the building. The white form of the house hovers on piles above the podium like an opaque plane, pierced by a number of discrete openings. A succession of spatial layers recedes from this surface to accommodate the house's principal volumes. The metal-faced front elevation that shields the living volume gives way on the north and west elevations to taut curtain walls that, together with the opaque front, reflect the interior layered space toward a small body of water to the southwest. Two sheets of water –a reflection pool and a swimming pool– penetrate the podium at the rear of the house. The swimming pool, plus a cube-shaped poolhouse and a low wall, effectively terminate the sitework at the western end.

Two separate stairs provide access to the three floors of the house; an enclosed spiral stair to the south and an open switchback stair to the north. This contrast between private and public circulation is echoed consistently in the organization of the volumes within. Thus, the public stair opening off the gallery foyer leads directly to the double-height living room on the first floor, while the cylindrical private stair ascends to the guest suite and library on the second floor and the master suite on the floor above. Two separate volumes on the third floor, a suspended study and an excercise room, afford views of the living volume and the garden. All glass walls that are exposed to low-angle western light are protected by electrically operated venetian blinds.

A ramped stair giving access from the swimming pool, a dog-leg stair to the roof terrace, and a two-car garage lodged under the guest suite on the south side of the house complete the symmetrical repertoire. The exterior of the house is clad in white enameled aluminum panels with aluminum fenestration and insulated glazing.

Photographs: Scott Frances / Esto Photographics

Site plan

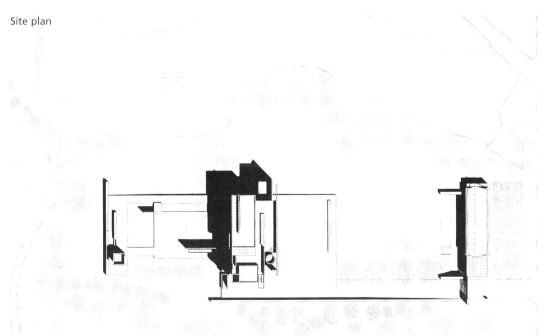

The stairways set the pace for both the building's interior and exterior. A metal structure following the progression of the wall provides access from the garden.

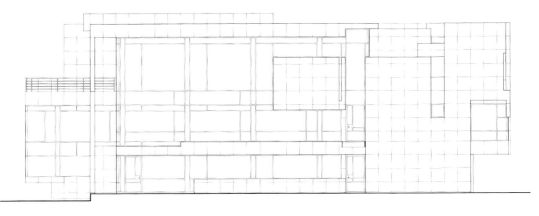

West elevation

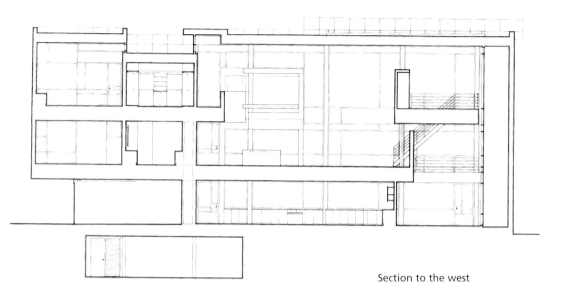

Section to the west

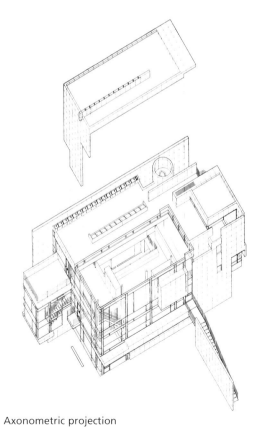

Axonometric projection

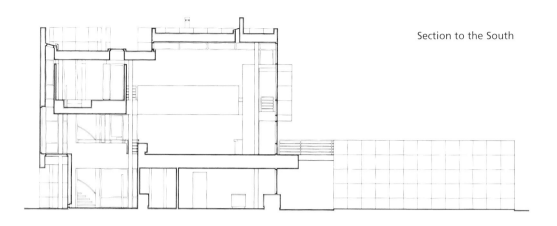

Section to the South

First floor plan

Second floor plan

Ground floor plan

Augustin + Frank
Viesel House
Falkensee, Germany

The project is situated outside of Berlin's city borders. Many of the inhabitants of Berlin nowadays move to the outskirts in search of a closer affinity to nature and with the desire to have their own house. This is also such a case. The clients, a married couple, run an antiquarian bookshop. The main turnover is made online, and for this reason they have decided to close the shop and move, with all the books, into the countryside.

The program for this building includes living space and work space for two persons, and the room for 370 running meters of books. In order to realize this project the architects planned a house which is 18 meters in length, and in breadth 6 meters on the ground floor and 7.5 in the upper story. The books are kept mainly on the upper floor. The house does not have a cellar because the ground-water level is high, and a raised ground floor level was not desired. The ground floor holds the weight of the whole book collection and is therefore solidly built using masonry and concrete. The upper story has been built over this, using a light timber frame construction. This separation has led to the house being able to be built very quickly. Whilst the ground floor was developed at the site itself, the upper story and windows were prefabricated in the workshop. In comparison with the surrounding buildings, the volume of the house is very large.

In order to compensate for this the architects have drawn it out lengthways, similar to the shape of the plot itself. In this manner the house gains a small garden and street elevations. From these sides, it is only possible to guess at the length to which the building stretches back. The large window openings are also on these sides.

From the neighboring plots, the building appears more closed. The lengthy outer wall, however, does not present itself as a homogeneous surface but rather is broken up by the effect of light and shade and by the filter of an open spaced larch boarding. With the exception of the wall at the entrance, which is set back, and of several reinforced concrete parts, all the exterior parts of the building are painted, or emulsified, with one color. The color is monochrome, and therefore the contrast between the fine details and the clear, simple contours of the building are accentuated. The building is situated at the intersection between town and countryside and should therefore contain elements of both. However, it should serve the purpose of familiarizing the occupants —former town-dwellers— with the country lifestyle.

In this case, the most important element is the projecting upper story. By use of this simple method, a space is created which serves a variety of purposes: a protected entrance, an anteroom leading to the kitchen and a space for outdoor activities which is protected from the rain.

Photographs: W. Huthmacher/ARTUR

The ground floor was built in-situ, while the first floor was made from prefabricated pieces lifted into place using a light wooden structure. This combination speeded up the construction process.

Site plan

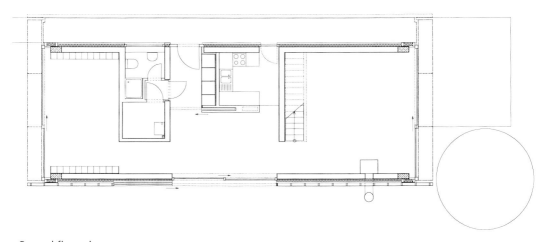

Ground floor plan

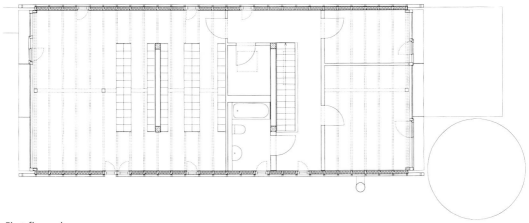

First floor plan

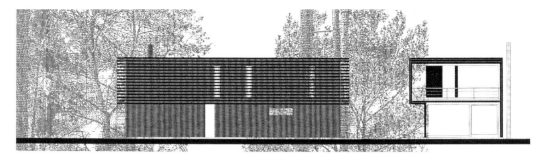

Elevation

The volume of this dwelling is very large in comparison with the buildings of the area. To compensate for this, it was attempted to lengthen its forms as far as possible, adapting them to the dimensions of the land.

Section

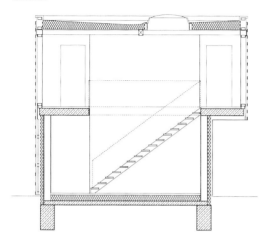

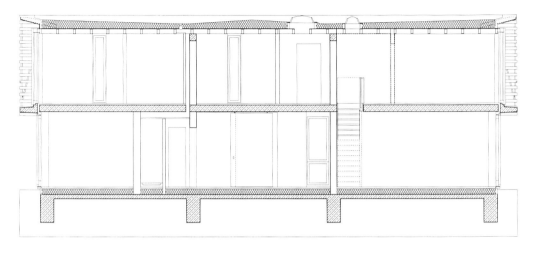